Unfading Beauty

By

Keith Sharp

TEACH Services, Inc.
PUBLISHING
www.TEACHServices.com • (800) 367-1844

World rights reserved. This book or any portion thereof may not be copied or reproduced in any form or manner whatever, except as provided by law, without the written permission of the publisher, except by a reviewer who may quote brief passages in a review.

The author assumes full responsibility for the accuracy of all facts and quotations as cited in this book. The opinions expressed in this book are the author's personal views and interpretations, and do not necessarily reflect those of the publisher.

This book is provided with the understanding that the publisher is not engaged in giving spiritual, legal, medical, or other professional advice. If authoritative advice is needed, the reader should seek the counsel of a competent professional.

_____

Copyright © 2000 Keith Sharp
Copyright © 2019 TEACH Services, Inc.
ISBN-13: 978-1-57258-161-1 (Paperback)

Library of Congress Control Number: 99-68902

Published by

www.TEACHServices.com • (800) 367-1844

Table of Contents

Lesson One:	A Comparable Helper	1
Lesson Two:	Wives	7
Lesson Three:	Mothers	11
Lesson Four:	Widows	17
Lesson Five:	Bible Teachers	23
Lesson Six:	In the Church	31
Lesson Seven:	A Symbol of Authority	37
Lesson Eight:	Modest Dress	45
Lesson Nine:	A Virtuous Woman	51
Lesson Ten:	Unfading Beauty	59
Lesson Eleven:	The Reward of Ruth	67
Lesson Twelve:	Esther	75
Lesson Thirteen:	Mary	85

Foreword

Virginia Scott Farish

Close to fifty years ago we went to worship one Lord's Day, in Del Rio, Texas. That day I made the acquaintance of the Harold F. Sharp family. Keith Sharp was there, a tiny baby in his mother's arms. Since that time the Sharp and Farish families have kept in reasonably close contact. I express my appreciation to Keith for asking me to write this foreword.

I have read his book and find it to be well written, true to the Word, and full of good advice, especially for older women who are instructed to teach the younger women to love their husbands and their children. This may seem to be repetitious as it is clearly stated in the Scriptures; but how many times do we read or "read over" these admonitions, know they are there, but never give any special thought to them; special thought such as, "is this intended for me?"

This book covers woman's work and responsibility in the sight of God, before she becomes a wife, while she is a wife, and when she has become a widow. It is remarkably free from opinions and faddish philosophy. It is a diligent gleaning from the Word of God of His instruction to those who would possess *Unfading Beauty*. It offers good material for reading, for pondering, for teaching and discussing in class settings. It is a pleasure to recommend it to the reader.

(The meeting of the Farish and Sharp families Sister Farish recalls took place in the fall of 1945. This foreword was written in 1996. Since then, Virginia Scott Farish, widow of Robert Farish and mother of Patrick Farish and his three brothers, has passed to her eternal reward. More than once I was the recipient of her hospitality and wisdom. She was indeed a godly mother in Israel.—KS)

Unfading Beauty
Introduction

The purpose of this workbook is to equip women to fulfill their peculiar gender role as women. It is not intended to be a study of the home, but, because it is a study of the peculiar feminine responsibilities, and woman was specifically formed by the Lord God to be man's complement in the marriage relationship, it will necessarily deal with woman's obligations in the home. The study will most definitely not be limited to these subjects.

I have striven to make the study general enough to be useful both in the United States and in societies not so much affected by Western thought. I have done this by concentrating on teaching the biblical principles of womanhood rather than dealing with human philosophies.

I recognize very well that I am a man writing about God's plan for women. This should not be a problem as long as I present what the Scriptures teach rather than my personal viewpoint. After all, the Scripture writers, who teach us all we know about the divine will for womanhood, were all men.

Many of the books written for women are of a devotional character. This book is intended to be a serious study of the Scriptures. I believe women have both the ability and responsibility to be serious Bible students. This volume will deal with issues that women face in all societies. The answers will be taken from the Bible.

Many popular books purporting to be scriptural studies for women are really the "power of positive thinking' popular psychology. They sometimes water down biblical demands or cast them in an unrealistically positive light. The Bible is ultimately the most positive book in existence for the faithful child of God, as it points the way to eternal life. And faithful adherence to its precepts produces joy and peace in the mind of mature Christians. But its demands of self sacrifice, submission and obedience and its condemnation of sin and sinners often are far from pleasant and positive. I have tried to avoid all popular psychology and simply present scriptural teaching on women.

Unless otherwise noted, all Scripture quotations and references are to the **New King James Version**. All questions in this workbook, as well as all questions that pertain to salvation, should ultimately be settled by an appeal to the inspired Word of God, the Bible.

The chapters consist of a lesson for all to read, a list of the passages used to encourage the students to concentrate on the biblical text, fact questions to test the students' mastery of the facts, thought questions to encourage personal application of the scriptural principles, and discussion questions to encourage the students to mutually help each other to a better understanding and application of the biblical truths. Some lessons contain terms to define. The definitions of these words or phrases will be given in the lesson.

I sought and received invaluable advice from Brethren James W. Adams, Edgar J. Dye, and Marshall Patton in preparation of chapters 5 and 6. I appreciate their help. As they know, I drew my own conclusions on the meaning of passages, and I alone should be held accountable for the material.

My wife, Sandy, taught this material to a class of young women in the congregation in Watertown, New York, and she and they made helpful suggestions. I am thankful to them.

May this little study be helpful to "women professing godliness" in their quest to be "partakers of the divine nature" and "heirs…of the grace of life."—the author

Lesson One:

A Comparable Helper

Lesson

And the Lord God said, "It is not good that man should be alone; I will make him a helper comparable to him." Out of the ground the Lord God formed every beast of the field and every bird of the air, and brought them to Adam to see what he would call them. And whatever Adam called each living creature, that was its name. So Adam gave names to all cattle, to the birds of the air, and to every beast of the field. But for Adam there was not found a helper comparable to him. And the Lord God caused a deep sleep to fall on Adam, and he slept; and He took one of his ribs, and closed up the flesh in its place. Then the rib which the Lord God had taken from man He made into a woman, and He brought her to the man. And Adam said: "This is now bone of my bones And flesh of my flesh; She shall be called Woman, Because she was taken out of Man." Therefore a man shall leave his father and mother and be joined to his wife, and they shall become one flesh. (Genesis 2:18–24)

It is a shock to the system of an American to journey to Africa and see the way women are commonly treated in African countries. In both pagan and Moslem societies men may have a plurality of wives, and women are characteristically thought of as the property and servants of men.

The opposite extreme is seen in America. In 1970 feminists forcibly occupied the offices of **Ladies Home Journal** magazine until they were given permission to print their views in that publication. The August, 1970 issue of the **Journal** carried an article entitled "The New Feminism," in which women's liberationists stated their philosophy. Among other things, they wrote:

Women's liberationists are united in a quest for total sexual equality and a rejection of the stifling restrictions imposed by masculine value….. Women come out of the house! You have everything to gain! (63,65)

These views, which seemed radical a quarter of a century ago, are now the accepted norm in Western society.

As is often the case, the scriptural truth is found between these extremes. What is the nature and role of women according to the Scriptures?

Woman's Special Purpose

In Genesis 2:18–24 Moses tells us how woman came to be. God recognized that man needed a companion. The Almighty purposed to give man the kind of companion he needed, a "helper comparable to him."

This phrase, "helper comparable," reveals woman's role and nature in relationship to man. In role she is his helper. Thus, man takes the lead, and woman assists him. In nature she is comparable to man. The term "comparable" is also translated "meet" (**KJV**) "answering to" (**ASV**, footnote) "suitable" (**NASB, NIV**) or "corresponding to." (**NASB**, footnote) It means "as over against, corresponding to, suitable for, meet." (Wilson. 271) The idea is "…agreeing with him mentally, physically, spiritually. She is not an inferior being." (Leupold. 1:130) In other words, she is his equal in nature. Thus, man's companion, given him by the Lord God, is in role his helper and in nature his equal.

The Lord caused the "beasts of the field" and "birds of the air" to pass by Adam, and the man named them. Thus, man was shown two things by an object lesson. Each of the animals had a companion, but Adam had none. The Lord demonstrated to Adam the need for companionship. But none of the animals was suitable to be man's companion. He needed a companion who shared his nature. No dog is suitable to be man's best friend!

Having shown Adam his need, God supplied that need. He took Adam's own flesh, his rib, and fashioned Eve from it and brought her to Adam to be his companion. Again, the Lord gave man an object lesson. Woman, being to man "bone of my bone and flesh of my flesh," has the same physical nature man has.

Further, she shares man's spiritual nature. God fashioned both male and female in His own image. (Genesis 1:27) This certainly does not mean they resemble God in fleshly appearance, for God is a Spirit (John 4:24), and a spirit has no physical form. (Luke 24:39) The woman as the man has a spirit within made in the likeness of God. Since the spirit is the seat of intellect (Ephesians 4:23), this implies that woman shares man's intellectual capacity. She likewise shares the opportunity to be an heir of the life in Christ. (1 Peter 3:7)

This equality of nature is not absolute or without exception. Rather, the woman is "comparable" or "corresponding to" man. Obviously, male and female are not identical physically, and the very passage that identifies woman as man's fellow heir of eternal life also describes her as "the weaker vessel." (1 Peter 3:7) Furthermore, while woman is just as intelligent as man, since she is more likely to be ruled by her emotions, a quality which beautifully adapts her for motherhood, she is more likely to be deceived than man and therefore less suited for the decision-making role. (2 Corinthians 11:3; 1 Timothy 2:14) Of course, both in the physical and spiritual realm, there are exceptions. Some women are physically stronger than their husbands, and some are less emotional.

In presenting Eve to Adam, the Lord God conducted the first wedding and began the institution of marriage. (verse 24) The relationship in which man is to enjoy his God-given companionship is marriage.

When He fashioned Eve from Adam's own rib, the Lord showed man that his closest earthly companion is his wife. Man's best friend is his wife. She fully satisfies his need for earthly companionship.

The First Sin

When man and woman first sinned, the woman led her husband into the sin. (Genesis 3:1–6) He was willingly led, but she took the lead. When the Lord God placed the curse upon woman for her part in this sin, He stated, "Your desire shall be for your husband, and He shall rule over you." (Genesis 3:16) She had usurped the leadership role, and so God emphatically stated her proper role. The Lord decreed that her desire will be to please her husband, and the husband was formally given the role of ruler in the home.

Roles and Responsibilities Peculiar to Womanhood Spring from Her Special Purpose

All of the New Testament teaching on the roles and responsibilities of women are based on her purpose in being created and her role in the first sin. Man is the head of woman (1 Corinthians 11:3) because woman was created from and for man. (1 Corinthians 11:8–9) Women are not to address the church as teachers over the assembly, because from the beginning God intended woman to be submissive. (1 Corinthians 14:34) Women are not to be teachers of the Bible over men, because Adam was created first and because Eve was deceived by Satan and Adam was not. (1 Timothy 2:11–14)

In Christ Jesus old distinctions pertaining to salvation are broken down. (Galatians 3:28) But this does not negate the fact that man is still the head of woman. (1 Corinthians 11:3)

Subjection Does Not Mean Inferiority

Worldly people incorrectly equate subjection with inferiority. The same verse that states man is the head of woman also declares that God is the head of Christ. (1 Corinthians 11:3) But Christ is equal in nature to His Father. (John 5:18) Subjection is simply a role to be filled and does not imply inferiority. In fact, greatness in the kingdom of God is not determined by being served but by serving others. (Matthew 20:25–28)

Biblical Application of the Principle of Subjection

The Lord does not leave women to guess where and when to apply the principle of feminine subjection. The wife is commanded to submit to her own husband. (Ephesians 5:22–24) Also, Christ gives males the lead in the local church. Women may not take the lead in the worship assembly where there are men present (1 Corinthians 14:34); nor may they in any other way be in authority over men in the local church (1 Timothy 2:12); and bishops, the leaders of the local church, must be men. (1 Timothy 3:1–2) But this does not mean women cannot take leadership roles in government , business, and social affairs. The principle of feminine subjection was true under the law (1 Corinthians 14:34; cf. Genesis 3:16), whereas godly Deborah was a judge of Israel (Judges 4:4–5), and faithful Queen Esther "wrote with full authority" the decree that instituted the feast of Purim for the entire Jewish people. (Esther 9:29,32) Also, Lydia, who was "faithful to the Lord," ran her own business. (Acts 16:14–15) Furthermore, in social affairs, women have the liberty to take leading roles. Martha exercised the lead in showing hospitality in the home she apparently shared with her sister Mary and her brother Lazarus. (Luke 10:38–40; cf. John 11:1–2; 12:1–2) Martha's mistake was in putting her hospitality ahead of hearing the Master, not in taking the leadership role in exercising hospitality. Women are admirably suited for planning and executing social events such as gatherings in the home and weddings. However, in every relationship, godly women maintain a "gentle and quiet" attitude. (1 Peter 3:3–4) Thus, the modern picture of the hard-driven, order-barking female executive going head to head with men is the opposite of the biblical ideal for women.

Conclusion

God designed woman for a special and important role, that of being man's companion, his suitable helper. That role especially applies to the marriage relationship, but it qualifies her attitudes and actions in other relationships as well. When a woman fills this role she can accomplish much good to the glory of God, the benefit of others, and her own salvation. Rather than seeking leadership or even equality in decision-making in the home and in the local church, godly women look for ways to serve that harmonize with and fulfill their sphere as "women professing godliness."

Questions

I. List of Passages Used in This Lesson (Read each passage and be able to discuss its meaning and its application to the lesson.)

Genesis 2:18–24	Galatians 3:28
Genesis 1:27	John 5:18
John 4:24	Matthew 20:25–28
Luke 24:39	Ephesians 5:22–24
Ephesians 4:23	1 Timothy 3:1–2
1 Peter 3:7	Judges 4:4–5
2 Corinthians 11:3	Esther 9:29,32
1 Timothy 2:11–14	Acts 16:14–15
Genesis 3:1–6	Luke 10:38–40
Genesis 3:16	John 11:1–2
1 Corinthians 11:3	John 12:1–2
1 Corinthians 11:8–9	1 Peter 3:3–4
1 Corinthians 14:34	

II. Term to Define

comparable

III. Fact Questions

1. Does man need a companion?
2. Are any animals suitable to be a companion for man?
3. What kind of companion does man need?
4. Who fulfills his need?
5. What is the meaning of the term "suitable"?
6. What is woman's nature?
7. Does woman share man's spiritual nature?
8. Are there limitations to woman's equality to man? If so, what are they?
9. What is her role?
10. In what relationship is this primarily fulfilled?
11. Who is a man's best friend?
12. How close is the husband-wife relationship?
13. Who led the way into the first sin?
14. What was the curse God placed on woman as the result of her part in the first sin?
15. Why do women have roles and responsibilities different from men?
16. Does the equality between men and women in Christ change this?
17. Does this mean men are better than women?
18. What determines greatness in the kingdom of God?
19. Should a woman submit to her husband?
20. Should she take a leadership role in the local church?
21. Is it right for a woman to be a government official?
22. May women be business executives?
23. What attitudes should she maintain at all times?

IV. Thought Questions

1. Should wives take the decision-making role over their husbands or share equally with them in that role?
2. Should women take the decision-making place in the local congregation or share with men in that place?
3. Should a man look down on his wife or on women generally as inferior to men?
4. Does the fact that the wife should try to please her husband mean he should not care about pleasing her? (cf. 1 Corinthians 7:33–34; Ephesians 5:25–31)
5. Is it always wrong for the wife to lead her husband? If not, how can you tell when it is right? (cf. Genesis 21:9–12)

V. Discussion

Let the women ask questions about practical problems they have in applying these principles in their daily lives.

List of Works Cited

The Bible, American Standard Version.
The Bible, King James Version.
The Bible, New American Standard Bible.
The Bible, New International Version.
Leupold, H.C., **Exposition of Genesis.**
Wilson, William, **Old Testament Word Studies.**

Lesson Two:

Wives

Lesson

Wives, submit to your own husbands, as to the Lord.
For the husband is head of the wife, as also Christ is head of the church; and He is the Savior of the body.
Therefore, just as the church is subject to Christ, so let the wives be to their own husbands in everything. (Ephesians 5:22–24)

While children are still preschoolers, the characteristic play of girls and boys becomes very different. Boys often play at sports or other rough games. Little girls seem drawn toward dolls and playing house. As girls grow older, they dream of their wedding day. They begin to make plans for the kind of house and furnishings they want. They are drawn toward being wives. As they grow up, get married, have children, and even after their children are grown, much more so than men, most women find fulfillment in their homes and families. This is the way God has made the woman.

God's commandments are always for our ultimate good. (1 John 5:3) God's will for woman coincides with what we observe concerning the keenest interest of most women. What then is God's plan for wives?

Becoming a Wife a Liberty

Do not misunderstand. If a woman decides to remain single and pursue a career outside the home, she is neither sinning nor being less spiritually minded than women who marry. Of course, some women remain single either because no man asks for them in marriage or the right man does not ask. The apostle Paul advised single women in Corinth to remain single. (1 Corinthians 7:8) By doing so it was easier for them to be faithful to Christ. (1 Corinthians 7:34) This was because there was persecution at Corinth at that time, and, in these circumstances, it would be difficult to remain loyal to the Lord while concerned about the welfare of a family. Even at that time, Paul did not command them to remain single but advised it. (1 Corinthians 7:6–8,25–28,38) The general rule is that marriage is preferable (1 Corinthians 7:2; 1 Timothy 5:14), but the apostle's advice in First Corinthians seven proves conclusively a woman may remain single without being less worthy. Young women who have their hearts set on marriage but for some reason have not found the right mate should use their lack of family responsibilities as an opportunity for increased service to the Lord. (1 Corinthians 7:34) It is far better to remain single than to marry a man who will bring misery or even lead his wife away from Christ. Or, as one young woman well said, "It's better to want what you don't have than to have what you don't want."

Submit to Her Husband

But when a woman marries, as most do, she takes upon herself three responsibilities. First, she is to "submit" or be "subject" to her own husband. (Ephesians 5:22–24) These two terms, "submit" and "is subject," are translated from the same Greek word, "*hupotasso*." (Vine. 4:86) The term is "primarily a military word" (Ibid) and means literally "to rank under." Its meaning is "*to subject one's self, to obey*, to submit to one's control." (Thayer. 645) In this passage it has the sense of "voluntary yielding in love." (Arndt & Gingrich. 855) A wife is not a slave. A slave may be forced to obey his master against the slave's own will. But wives are to willingly yield to the rule of their own husbands through love, even as the bride of Christ, His church, willingly, lovingly submits to His will. Thus, she will not rebel against his rule or scheme to secretly circumvent his decisions. Her obedience is voluntary submission. The husband has no authority to force her into submission. Christ does not beat His bride into subjection. In this willing, loving submission she fulfills her divinely ordained role as a "helper comparable" to man. (Genesis 2:18) She should show respect to her husband, even as the church is to reverence her husband, Christ. (Ephesians 5:33) Thus, wives should be respectful in the way they talk to and about their husbands. The only reason the wife should disobey her husband is if his rule contradicts God's will. (Colossians 3:18; Acts 5:29)

Love Her Husband

Responsibilities of Wives

- Submit to Her Husband
- Love Her Husband
- Be a Homemaker

The apostle Paul directs aged women to "admonish the young women to love their husbands." (Titus 2:4) Most young women do not have to be directed to have romantic love to their husbands, nor can someone manufacture emotional attachment in obedience to a command. Rather, the older women are to counsel younger women how they demonstrate their love for their husbands. A wife shows love to her husband by seeking to please him rather than herself. (1 Corinthians 7:34) She will not nag him to get her own way or to change him to suit herself. (Proverbs 19:13; 21:9,19) Wives face a special temptation to so misuse the tongue. Generally the wife is physically weaker than her husband. She might be tempted to use her tongue as a weapon to get her own way, nagging him until in frustration he gives in to her desire. This is a form of rebellion against his authority. Further, she will strive to fulfill his sexual needs and never use the withdrawal of the bed as a means of punishment or to accomplish her own will. (1 Corinthians 7:2–5) The wife belongs to her husband, and he belongs to her. She will never defile herself with another man. (Hebrews 13:4; Proverbs 12:4) Often, godly women face the problem of having an unbelieving husband. Wives in this difficult situation should live submissive, pure, gentle, quiet lives, so as to win their husbands to the Lord by the example of Christ living in them. (1 Peter 3:1–4)

Be a Homemaker

The apostle also teaches older women to admonish young women to be "homemakers." (Titus 2:4–5) This word means "keeping at home and taking care of household affairs." (Thayer. 442) This is not to say a woman cannot have a career. Faithful Lydia ran her own business. (Acts 16:14–15) But when a woman marries, she has chosen her career, that of a homemaker. Nor does it mean a married woman cannot work outside the home. The mother of King Lemuel described the "virtuous wife" as one who dealt in real estate, gardening, and making and selling clothing. (Proverbs 31:16,24) But work outside the home must be subordinate to and not interfere with her primary career, that of a homemaker. In my opinion, the biggest hindrance to most married women in fulfilling their homemaking responsibilities is the love of money, both on the part of the wife and the husband. Many couples are not content to live on the income of the husband alone because they desire more material possessions. They need to learn to be content rather than greedy. (1 Timothy 6:6–10)

The work of a homemaker is to "manage the house." (1 Timothy 5:14) This phrase is literally translated "house despot (ruler)" and refers to the management and direction of household affairs. Joseph, though a young man, did this work in Potiphar's house when Potiphar "made him overseer of his house, and all that he had he put in his hand." So complete was Joseph's superintendence of Potiphar's affairs, though Joseph was Potiphar's servant, that Potiphar "left all that he had in Joseph's hand, and he did not know what he had except for the bread which he ate." (Genesis 39:1–6) The skills Joseph learned in this work qualified him to be the ruler of Egypt, second only to Pharaoh. The virtuous wife of Proverbs watched "over the ways of her household." (Proverbs 31:10, 27) Arrogant men and women's liberationists picture homemaking as "mindless drudgery." Do you think Joseph was a "mindless drudge?" Does Proverbs picture a stupid slave? The role of a wife in the home is like a hired city manager with a city council. The city council sets policy and determines a budget, possibly with the advice of the city manager, and the city manager carries out that policy within the budget set by the council. The husband, the head of the family, should determine, with the advice of his wife, the direction the family is to take, and she should carry out those decisions in the home. She has the work of providing an attractive, comfortable place to live; feeding the family nourishing, pleasant meals; caring for children; managing a household on a budget; and on and on. No wonder aged women must teach young women how to do this.

Conclusion

The role of a wife is demanding. The virtuous wife demonstrates self-sacrifice (Proverbs 31:10–12), hard work (Proverbs 31:13–19,22,24) and wisdom. (Proverbs 31:16,26–27) But the rewards of this career can be even greater.

> *Her children rise up and call her blessed;*
> *Her husband also, and he praises her:*
> *"Many daughters have done well,*
> *But you excel them all."*
> *Charm is deceitful and beauty is passing,*
> *But a woman who fears the Lord, she shall be praised.*
> *Give her of the fruit of her hands,*
> *And let her own works praise her in the gates.*
> (Proverbs 31:28–31)

Questions

I. List of Passages Used in This Lesson (Read each passage and be able to discuss its meaning and its application to the lesson.)

Ephesians 5:22–24	Titus 2:4–5
1 John 5:3	Proverbs 19:13
1 Corinthians 7:6–8	Proverbs 21:9,19
1 Corinthians 7:25–28	Hebrews 13:4
1 Corinthians 7:34	Proverbs 12:4
1 Corinthians 7:38	1 Peter 3:1–4
1 Corinthians 7:2–5	Acts 16:14–15
1 Timothy 5:14	Proverbs 31:16,24
Genesis 2:18	1 Timothy 6:6–10
Ephesians 5:33	Genesis 39:1–6
Colossians 3:18	Proverbs 31:10–31
Acts 5:29	

II. Terms to Define

1. submit

2. is subject

3. homemakers

4. manage the house

III. Fact Questions

1. Is God's plan for wives for the good of women?

2. Is it wrong for a woman to remain single?

3. Should a wife submit to her husband?

4. How does she do this?

5. When should she not submit to him?

6. How does the wife show love to her husband?

7. Is it a sin for a woman to have a career outside the home?

8. Is it a sin for a married woman to have work outside the home?

9. Why do so many wives have outside jobs?

10. What are the three responsibilities of a wife?

11. Is the role of a wife difficult?

12. Does it require self-sacrifice?

13. Does it require hard work?

14. Does it take wisdom?

IV. Thought Questions

1. How should a woman determine whether or not to get married?

2. How can a young woman learn how to show love to her husband?

3. If your husband is not a Christian, what is the best way to try to lead him to Christ?

4. How should a married woman decide whether or not to take a job outside the home?

5. How does a young woman learn how to be a homemaker?

V. Discussion

Make a list of all the specific jobs involved in managing the house. Compare your list to those of others in the class.

List of Works Cited

Arndt, W.F. and F.W. Gingrich, **A Greek-English Lexicon of the New Testament.**
Thayer, J.H., **A Greek-English Lexicon of the New Testament**
Vine, W.E., **An Expository Dictionary of New Testament Words**

Lesson Three:

Mothers

Lesson

that they admonish the young women to love their husbands, to love their children, to be discreet, chaste, homemakers, good, obedient to their own husbands, that the word of God may not be blasphemed. (Titus 2:4–5)

Mothers and motherhood have been the objects of praise in every land and in every age. Proverbial statements of the eminent value of good mothers are too numerous to cite them all. An anonymous, well known statement is "The hand that rocks the cradle rules the world." Emerson well stated, "Men are what their mothers have made them." But, mothers, do you live up to these eloquent tributes? To help you answer this penetrating question, we inquire, "What is God's plan for mothers?"

The Desire for Motherhood Is Proper

Even unbelieving feminists have been forced to recognize that the desire to have a baby and to nurture children is firmly imbedded in the nature of women. Perhaps no need is more deep seated and universal in the female gender. Little girls enjoy taking care of baby dolls. Women thrill to hold and cuddle a new baby. This desire is normal and good. The apostle to the Gentiles wrote, "Therefore I desire that the younger widows marry, bear children, manage the house, give no opportunity to the adversary to speak reproachfully." (1 Timothy 5:14) The psalmist praises the Lord's care of the downtrodden thus: "He grants the barren woman a home, Like a joyful mother of children. Praise the Lord!" (Psalm 113:9)

Love the Controlling Emotion

> **MOTHERS**
>
> **"Love their children"**
>
> ♥ RAISE THEM HERSELF
> ♥ IMPART FAITH to THEM
> ♥ DO NOT SHOW PARTIALITY

In harmony with woman's emotional constitution and the needs of young children, her relationship with her children is dominated and guided by an emotion—love. Woman, with her tender heart, gentle touch, and softer form, is perfectly fashioned by the Lord to express love to children. The depth and strength of motherly love has always been a source of wonder and admiration to thoughtful men. The older women are to teach the younger women "to love their children." (Titus 2:4) The word "love" in this passage is from the Greek word "*philoteknos.*" This is a combination word, putting together the Greek terms "*philos*" (love) and "*teknos*" (child), and means "*loving one's offspring* or *children.*" (Thayer. 655) Vine says that the verb "*phileo,*" in contrast with the more common New Testament Greek word "*agapao,*" "more nearly represents tender affection." (Vine. 3:21) Tender affection toward her children is the inherent emotion of a mother. In fact, so intense and self-sacrificing is that natural love that wise Solomon used it as the means to discern the real mother of a child, when two women both laid claim to him. The real mother would rather renounce her claim to the child than to see him harmed. Though an harlot, the woman "yearned with compassion for her son." (1 Kings 3:16–27) But, while this emotion is natural, the knowledge of how best to express it, how best to mother a child, is not. This is what older, godly women are to teach young women.

Love of Mothers Properly Expressed

How, then, should a mother express her love for her children? First, by raising them herself rather than turning them over to a baby-sitter or day care center. Paul admonishes the young widows to "marry, bear children, manage the house." (1 Timothy 5:14) Older women are to teach young women to be homemakers. (Titus 2:4) Mothers who sacrifice the personal care of their children for a job outside the home are both failing in a paramount responsibility and missing perhaps the most important, personally fulfilling opportunity they will ever have—the opportunity to nurture and guide the little ones in the most formative period of their lives. Sister Virgie Bell of Baytown, Texas, herself the wife of a retired elder and the mother of four faithful daughters, gave me this beautiful poem, whose author we do not know.

I took a piece of plastic clay
And idly fashioned it one day.
And as my fingers pressed it still,
It moved and yielded to my will.
I came again when days were passed,
The bit of clay was hard at last.
The form I gave it still it bore,
But I could change it never more.

I took a piece of living clay
And gently formed it day by day.
And molded it with power and art,
A young child's soft and yielding heart.
I came again when years were gone,
It was a man I looked upon.
He still the early impress wore,
And I could change it nevermore.

What kind of adult will your child be if his character is molded by worldly, unbelieving baby sitters, the immorality of television, and the constant companionship of other children whose filthy mouths are a reflection of the ungodly homes in which they live? Would you entrust jewelry to the person to whom you entrust your child? Can any amount of money and worldly possessions replace the opportunity to nurture and guide your child or give you solace should he lose his soul? They grow up so quickly, and the opportunity to be with them in their tender years can never be regained once sacrificed. The wisest mere mortal who ever lived observed, "a child left to himself brings shame to his mother." (Proverbs 29:15) If you do not mold the child into the image of Christ, who will?

When the daughter of Pharaoh saw the helpless infant Moses hidden in the ark among the reeds, her feminine heart melted with compassion, and she adopted him as her own son. But she sought a nurse to raise him, and Moses' older sister Miriam, watching the proceedings, cleverly volunteered their mother for the job. When Moses was grown, his loyalty lay not with the Egyptians, the people of his adoptive mother, but with Israel, the people of his nurse and birth mother. (Exodus 2:1–12; Acts 7:20–25) Although Moses received all the education available to an Egyptian of royal descent, the training received as an infant and toddler at the breast of his nurse was that which determined his character and loyalty. Whose influence will determine the character and loyalty of your child?

This love is best expressed when a mother gives her child the most precious gift he can ever receive, a gift that no money can buy, the gift of faith. When aged Paul wrote his last letter, the second letter to his beloved son in the faith Timothy, he remembered tenderly the "genuine faith" of Timothy and noted where Timothy received that faith—"which dwelt first in your grandmother Lois and your mother Eunice." (2 Timothy 1:5)

How does a mother impart faith to her child? He does not inherit her faith, as he might receive the color of her eyes or the shape of her nose. Timothy's grandmother Lois and his mother Eunice imparted faith to him by teaching him "from childhood…the Holy Scriptures." (2 Timothy 3:14–15) When my father, H.F. Sharp, was a small child he worked alongside his mother, whom I called "Mama Sharp," pulling grass in the vegetable garden. She pacified him by telling him the stories of the great Old Testament characters. They became more than names; they came to life in his mind. Several people have told me he was the best preacher they ever heard in preaching from the Old Testament. The reason may be traced to a vegetable garden and a little tot pulling grass with his mother.

Mothers also impart faith and godly character by living these qualities before their children. Children are the best mimics in the world. And the people they imitate the most are their parents. We have a saying, "Like father, like son." That is "chimney corner scripture"; it's not in the Bible. The Bible says, in speaking of apostate Judah, "Like mother, like daughter" (Ezekiel 16:44) and "You are your mother's daughter." (verse 45) Mothers, if you want your children to grow up to be Christ-like, Christ must live in you before them.

Furthermore, mothers give their children faith and godly character by correcting and punishing them when they do wrong. Some may say, "But I love them too much to spank them!" Solomon replies, "He who spares his rod hates his son, But he who loves him disciplines him promptly." (Proverbs 13:24) When we do not punish our children for misbehavior, we are teaching them that bad actions do not have bad consequences. When will they learn otherwise—in school, from a civil court, or before the judgment bar of God? Pity the poor mother with small, out-of-control children in the supermarket. She is a nervous, exhausted wreck. What can she do? "Correct your son, and he will give you rest; Yes, he will give delight to your soul." (Proverbs 29:17) Don't yell and scream. They just learn to "tune you out." Don't make idle threats you have no intention of carrying out. You are lying to them, and they know it. Spank them. I did not say to brutalize them. I did not say to abuse them. Corrective discipline is an expression of love. Our heavenly Father loves us, so He chastens us. (Hebrews 12:6) One can administer pain without inflicting injury.

A mother who loves her children will not be partial to one child over others. "Esau was a skillful hunter, a man of the field," whereas his younger twin, Jacob, "was a mild man, dwelling in tents." (Genesis: 27) Isaac, their father, was partial to Esau, whereas Rebekah, their mother, loved Jacob more. (verse 28) Rebekah led Jacob into deceiving his aged, blind father to think he was Esau, so Jacob received the blessing Isaac intended to give Esau. As the result, Esau hated Jacob and awaited their father's death as the opportune time to kill him. Rebekah had to help her son flee for his life. So far as the inspired Word records, Rebekah never saw Jacob again. (Genesis 27:1–45) The partiality to one son over another these parents manifested caused the father to rebel against God's prophetic choice of Jacob, the mother to help her son deceive his father, one son to hate the other and determine to kill him, and the other son to become a deceiver and to flee for his life, permanently separating him from his parents. What a price for partiality.

Finally, the mother who loves her children will gladly work the long, difficult labor, demeaned by the world as mindless drudgery, that it takes to be a good mother. Yes, if you stay home and take care of your children, you are working, and you do have a full time job, yes, a career.

> *She seeks wool and flax,*
> *And willingly works with her hands.*
> *She is like the merchant ships,*
> *She brings her food from afar.*
> *She also rises while it is yet night,*
> *And provides food for her household,*
> *And a portion for her maidservants.*

> *She considers a field and buys it;*
> *From her profits she plants a vineyard.*
> *She girds herself with strength,*
> *And strengthens her arms.*
> *She perceives that her merchandise is good,*
> *And her lamp does not go out by night.*
> *She stretches out her hands to the distaff,*
> *And her hand holds the spindle.*
> *She extends her hand to the poor,*
> *Yes, she reaches out her hands to the needy.*
> *She is not afraid of snow for her household,*
> *For all her household is clothed with scarlet.*
> *She makes tapestry for herself;*
> *Her clothing is fine linen and purple.*
> *Her husband is known in the gates,*
> *When he sits among the elders of the land.*
> *She makes linen garments and sells them,*
> *And supplies sashes for the merchants.*
> *Strength and honor are her clothing;*
> *She shall rejoice in time to come.*
> *She opens her mouth with wisdom,*
> *And on her tongue is the law of kindness.*
> *She watches over the ways of her household,*
> *And does not eat the bread of idleness.* (Proverbs 31:13–27)

Does that sound like a mindless drudge?

Conclusion

It is hard to imagine a role one could occupy that has more potential for good and personal fulfillment and is more praiseworthy than motherhood. It should not be surprising that men have through the ages heaped such adulation on mothers. Perhaps the most beautiful I have ever read was from the pen of James R. Cope, former President of Florida College, in tribute to his own mother on the occasion of her 84th birthday.

> *That's my mother. September 18 is her 84th birthday. Not alert as she once was and almost blind, she lives near Cookeville, Tennessee, with my sister who tenderly cares for her. Her form is stooped and weakened, her brow creviced. Silver threads run majestically among the chestnut locks which my baby fingers caressed more than fifty years ago. Tired and wrinkled hands, once callused by physical toil in kitchen, vegetable garden, lawn, and even the barn before she taught me how to milk the cows, bespeak a heart that lost sight of self in loving service for those she mothered. And flowers, always flowers, flowers everywhere! Those hands loved to plant them as she bestowed the beauty of her soul upon the landscape for others to enjoy.*

> *When I saw her last, I studied carefully those hands that never wrought evil to any man, woman, or child. I was reminded of the poem, "Beautiful Hands," by Ellen M.H. Gatos. I share it here with you, dear reader.*

> > *"Such beautiful, beautiful hands,*
> > *they're neither white nor small,*
> > *And you, I know, would scarcely think*
> > *That they were fair at all.*
> > *I've looked on hands whose form and hue*

*A sculptor's dream might be,
Yet these are aged, wrinkled hands
Most beautiful to me.*

*"Such beautiful, beautiful hands,
Though heart were weary and sad
those patient hands kept toiling on
That the children might be glad.
I almost weep when looking back
To childhood's distant day!
I think how these hands rested not
When children were at their play.*

*"Such beautiful, beautiful hands!
They're growing feeble now,
And time and pain have left their mark
On head, and heart and brow.
Alas! Alas! the nearing time—
And the sad, sad day to me,
when "neath the daisies, out of sight,
Those hands must folded be.*

*"But, oh! beyond the shadowy lands,
Where all is bright and fair,
I know full well those dear old hands
Will palms of victory bear;
Where crystal streams, through sadless years
Flow over golden sands,
And where the old are young again,
I'll clasp my mother's hands."*

Mothers, so live that such a tribute may be yours from husband, children, and the great Judge of all.

"Her children rise up and call her blessed;
Her husband also, and he praises her." (Proverbs 31:28)

Questions

I. List of Passages Used in This Lesson (Read each passage and be able to discuss its meaning and its application to the lesson.)

Titus 2:4–5
1 Timothy 5:14
Psalm 113:9
1 Kings 3:16–27
Proverbs 29:15
Exodus 2:1–12
Acts 7:20–25
2 Timothy 1:5

2 Timothy 3:14–15
Ezekiel 16:44–45
Proverbs 13:24
Proverbs 29:17
Hebrews 12:6
Genesis 25:27–28
Genesis 27:1–45
Proverbs 31:13–28

II. Phrase to Define
    love her children

III. Fact Questions

1. Is it proper for a young woman to desire to have a baby?

2. What principle should govern a mother's relationship with her children?

3. Is this emotion natural to a mother?

4. Is knowing how to properly express this emotion natural?

5. Should a mother let someone else raise her children while she goes out into the workplace?

6. Should mothers impart faith to their children?

7. How do they do this?

8. Is it right to have a favorite child that is given preferential treatment over the others?

9. Is being a good mother hard work?

10. Does it require wisdom?

11. Do the rewards of being a good mother justify the efforts and sacrifices?

IV. Thought Questions

1. Are there circumstances in which it is right for a mother to turn the care of her small children over to someone else? What would these circumstances be?

2. Are there acceptable alternatives to spanking as corrective discipline for children? If so, what and under what circumstances?

3. How old does a child have to be before he should be punished for misbehavior?

4. What should a mother do when her child misbehaves in the worship assembly?

5. What rewards does good motherhood bring?

V. Discussion

1. Make a list of the different jobs involved in being a mother. Compare your list with those of others in the class.

2. What are some good methods of teaching the Bible and scriptural principles to children?

3. Do you know some good literature for teaching children biblical truths that you can share with the class?

4. What biblical facts should children commit to memory?

5. Do you have suggestions how to get them to memorize these facts?

List of Works Cited

Thayer, J.H., **A Greek-English Lexicon of the New Testament**
Vine, W.E., **An Expository Dictionary of New Testament Words**

Lesson Four:

Widows

Lesson

In 1994 in the United States the life expectancy of men was 72.3 years and that of women was 79 years. There were 32 million people over the age of 65, of whom 9.52 million lived alone. Eight of ten of those over age 65 living alone were women. In that same year there were 11.1 million widows in the U.S. and 2.2 million widowers. Obviously widowhood, though a prospect many women are loathe to contemplate, is something they need to consider objectively before it becomes a present reality. Furthermore, all Christians should be aware of the problems attendant to widowhood and the scriptural solutions to them. What problems are common to widows, and how does the Lord teach us to meet them?

Old Testament

Widows were obviously relatively helpless in that they had lost the husband upon whom they depended for support. In ancient times there usually was no honorable occupation a woman could pursue other than home making, and even today godly widows who have properly spent years working in the home are ill equipped to make a living for themselves and unprepared to face the clever cruelty of a business world driven by heartless greed. Often times the debilitating effects of old age compound these problems.

In every age, God has required that His people care for the poor and helpless, including widows. Job described the wicked as those who "take the widow's ox as a pledge." (Job 24:3) He maintained his own righteousness before God as one who provided help for the poor, the fatherless and widows. (31:16–18)

Responsibilities of Israelites to Widows

✡ **Do Justice**

✡ **Leave Gleanings**

✡ **Give Third Year Tithe**

In the law of Moses, the Lord taught Israel to be compassionate toward those who were helpless and easily oppressed. Three categories of people were repeatedly mentioned as fitting this description: the fatherless (orphans), widows and strangers (foreigners who lived among them). (e.g., Deuteronomy 10:18) Moses taught them that God provided justice for and loved these easily oppressed people and that they were to do the same. As an inducement to treat the helpless among them justly and kindly, He directed them to remember their helpless condition as strangers in Egypt and how the Egyptians oppressed them. (Deuteronomy 10:19)

The law gave Israelites certain specific obligations toward these defenseless groups. Most basically, God's Old Covenant people were to see that those unable to procure justice for themselves, including widows, received just treatment. (Deuteronomy 24:17–18) Those who perverted justice due the widow were cursed. (27:19) It would be easy to oppress them, as they had none to plead their cause and could not bribe a corrupt judge into rendering justice for them, so Israel was specifically commanded not to oppress them. (Exodus 22:21–22) Isaiah thus condemned the apostate Northern Kingdom:

Woe to those who decree unrighteous decrees, Who write misfortune, Which they have prescribed To rob the needy of justice, And to take what is right from the poor of My people, That widows may be their prey, And that they may rob the fatherless.
(Isaiah 10:1–2; cf. 1:21–23)

He admonished them to "Plead for the widow." (1:16–17) Jeremiah warned backsliding Judah to stop oppressing "the stranger, the fatherless, and the widow." (Jeremiah 7:5–7) Zechariah informed the Jews of the Restoration that God had sent their fathers into captivity because they refused to heed the warning to "not oppress the widow or the fatherless, the alien or the poor." (Zechariah 7:8–14) The Lord scathingly denounced the Jewish rulers of His day:

Woe to you, scribes and Pharisees, hypocrites! For you devour widows' houses, and for a pretense make long prayers. Therefore you will receive greater condemnation.
(Matthew 23:14)

Business men who take advantage of the aged widows to line their pockets with the meager savings of the poor are low indeed. Even lower are lawyers and judges who uphold the wicked schemes of these rich scoundrels because of their money. But the lowest of all are those, such as preachers who beg for money on television and religious leaders who gain the confidence of the elderly to get their money, who use the pretense of religious piety to rob elderly widows of the pittance on which they depend.

But those who were left without the means to make a living could starve even if not mistreated. So the Lord commanded individual Israelites to provide sustenance for them. Yet that sustenance was not in the form of a give away program but was designed to require the poor to work for their food. God intends that all who are capable of work either do so or do without the necessities of life. (2 Thessalonians 3:8,10) Honest toil is not a curse but a blessing , as it gives purpose and dignity to the one so employed. (Genesis 2:15) No righteous person desires to be a burden to others. (2 Thessalonians 3:8) Those who have no work of their own find themselves led into sin and sinful meddling into the affairs of others. (2 Thessalonians 3:11; 1 Timothy 5:13) Thus, the law required that Jews not glean their fields after they had been harvested but allow the widows, orphans, and poor foreigners living among them to come into their harvested fields and glean what had been left for their sustenance. (Deuteronomy 24:19–22) Thus, the poor received sustenance, but they were given the dignity of work and were not a burden. Faithful Ruth gleaned in the field of Boaz to provide food for herself and her mother-in-law, Naomi. (Ruth chapter 2) Rather than degrading her, such menial work brought this poor widow and foreigner a good name in Israel. (Ruth 2:8–13) Elijah miraculously provided food for a poor widow of Zarephath, a Gentile, and she in turn fed Elijah and gave him a place to stay as he hid from Ahab and Jezebel. (1 Kings 17:8–16; cf. Luke 4:25–26)

To supplement this provision, Israelites were to show their love and care for the "Levite, the stranger, the fatherless, and the widow" by giving them a tithe (tenth) of their produce every third year as a gift. This was made a condition of God blessing them with abundant produce in the land. (Deuteronomy 14:28–29; 26:12–15)

Honor Father and Mother

The fifth commandment of the Ten Commandments of the law and the first in human to human relations, as the basis for an orderly society, was "Honor your father and your mother." (Exodus 20:12; Deuteronomy 5:16) This necessarily implied that a child was to support his parents, including his widowed mother, when they were aged and unable to care for themselves. (Matthew 15:1–6; Mark 7:5–13) The scribes and Pharisees dishonored their parents and broke the law of God by claiming that their contribution to the temple replaced their responsibility to their parents. Christians have the same responsibility to honor our parents (Ephesians 6:2–3), including the obligation to support them when they are unable to do so themselves. (1 Timothy 5:4) This is not a matter of grace, that is favor to the undeserving, but of showing our respect to those to whom it is due by right and making a small, partial repayment for their sacrifices when we were children. (Ibid)

It is a universal tendency to shift responsibility. Individuals often want congregations to assume their responsibilities, and congregations often send contributions to distant human organizations and think they have met their obligations. Children must not shove their obligations to their parents upon the church, and the church must not accept these responsibilities. (1 Timothy 5:4,8,16) Likewise churches have no authority to send contributions to any human organization, benevolent or otherwise.

New Testament

The New Testament as well as the Old makes provisions for widows. In addition to the obligation children have to honor their parents, the church is charged with the care of certain widows. The church at Jerusalem daily distributed to widows among them. (Acts 6:1) Christians demonstrate pure religion by seeing to the needs of orphans and widows. (James 1:27)

The most comprehensive passage in the Bible on widows is 1 Timothy 5:3–16.

Honor widows who are really widows. But if any widow has children or grandchildren, let them first learn to show piety at home and to repay their parents; for this is good and acceptable before God. Now she who is really a widow, and left alone, trusts in God and continues in supplications and prayers night and day. But she who lives in pleasure is dead while she lives. And these things command, that they may be blameless. But if anyone does not provide for his own, and especially for those of his household, he has denied the faith and is worse than an unbeliever. Do not let a widow under sixty years old be taken into the number, and not unless she has been the wife of one man, well reported for good works: if she has brought up children, if she has lodged strangers, if she has washed the saints' feet, if she has relieved the afflicted, if she has diligently followed every good work. But refuse the younger widows; for when they have begun to grow wanton against Christ, they desire to marry, having condemnation because they have cast off their first faith. And besides they learn to be idle, wandering about from house to house, and not only idle but also gossips and busybodies, saying things which they ought not. Therefore I desire that the younger widows marry, bear children, manage the house, give no opportunity to the adversary to speak reproachfully. For some have already turned aside after Satan. If any believing man or woman has widows, let them relieve them, and do not let the church be burdened, that it may relieve those who are really widows.

Verse three introduces the subject, the church should honor those who are really widows ("widows indeed," **KJV**). The word "widow" literally means "bereft." (Arndt & Gingrich. 889) To "honor" such an one is to give her "respect and material assistance." (Vine. 2:231; cf. verses 16–17; Matthew 15:4–6; Mark 7:8–13)

Verses three through eight discuss widows who have relatives who can care for them. A widow, though her husband is dead, is not really bereft of family to whom she can look for support if she has children or grandchildren. Her children and grandchildren should pay her back in small measure for the many sacrifices she made for them while they were young and should learn to show proper reverence and devotion at home by supporting her. The widow with relatives is in contrast with one who is truly desolate of kin and can only look to God in prayer for her sustenance (the widow indeed). Nor should the church support the widow who has given herself to a life of pleasure rather than to good works. Those family members who would not support a widowed mother, grandmother or aunt have in practice denied the faith, which demands that we honor our parents, and do not even measure up to unbelievers in the world, most of whom recognize the responsibilities they have to their aged relatives.

In verses nine and ten the apostle describes those who are really widows and are to be enrolled into the number of widows to be supported at the expense of the local church. They are at least sixty years old, have been married only once (This may simply refer to being scripturally married) and have engaged in such good works as raising children (either her own or others), keeping traveling Christians (cf. Hebrews 13:2; 3 John 5–8), practicing hospitality (cf. Luke 7:44–46; 1 Peter 4:9), relieving the afflicted, and diligently performing other good works. (cf. Matthew 25:35–36; Acts 9:36–39)

Some practical observations are in order. As young men should begin in their youth developing the character that would eventually qualify them to be elders of the church, young women should begin in youth doing the works and developing the character that some day might give them the right to be enrolled by the church as a widow indeed. Although it cannot be proven that widows indeed constitute a group who are to do work in behalf of the local church, certainly a widow who has always engaged in these good works will continue to do so as long as she is physically able. She also will labor not to be a burden. Being supported by the church will enable her to have the financial resources to continue these good works and will free her from the necessity of seeking secular employment that would limit her time to engage in good works. From such godly women there might be those perfectly suited to teach young women how to properly fulfill their family obligations. (Titus 2:3–5)

Verses eleven through fifteen reveal why younger widows (those under sixty), even though they may be godly, are not to be enrolled by the church as widows indeed. They will "feel sensual desires in disregard of Christ." (verse 11, **NASB**) These normal impulses might lead them, in their desire for the fulfillment properly available in marriage, to cast off the faith by engaging in immorality. Further, they are tempted to be idle and thus to become busy bodies and gossips. Thus, the best course for younger widows, and young women generally, is to marry and find productive employment and fulfillment in the duties of homemaking and raising children. Indeed, the apostle observes, some had already fallen prey to the temptations attendant to the single life.

Verse sixteen is a summary. Christians should support those widows who are their family obligations, and the church is limited to supporting widows indeed.

Three Needs—All Met

A consideration of the teaching of the Scriptures reveals that the Lord recognizes three needs that widows have in common with other people, needs that may be difficult for them to meet, and makes provision for their fulfillment. Widows have material needs. Whereas the local church is limited to those who qualify as "really widows" in their relief work, the families of other widows should assist them, and Christians should be concerned to help any deserving needy, including widows, when they are presented with the opportunity. (Acts 6:1; 1 Timothy 5:3–16; James 1:27) Widows need love and companionship.

WIDOWS NEEDS ALL MET

📖 MATERIAL NEEDS

- ☛ REALLY WIDOWS: LOCAL CHURCH—1 Timothy 5:3, 9–10, 16
- ☛ WIDOWS with FAMILY: FAMILY—1 Timothy 5:4, 8, 16
- ☛ OTHER WIDOWS: CHRISTIANS—James 1:27

📖 LOVE and COMPANIONSHIP

- ☛ YOUNG WIDOWS: MARRIAGE—1 Timothy 5:14
- ☛ WIDOWS with FAMILY: FAMILY—1 Timothy 5:4
- ☛ OTHER WIDOWS: OTHER CHRISTIANS—Romans 12:9–10

📖 RESPECT and DIGNITY OF SELF-WORTH

- ☛ ALL WOMEN: EARN—1 Timothy 5:9–10
- ☛ WIDOWS with FAMILY: FAMILY—Timothy 5:4
- ☛ REALLY WIDOWS: CHURCH—1 Timothy 5:3

Thus, younger widows should seek marriage, the family of older widows should shower them with love, and all Christians in the local church should show love and concern for each other. (1 Timothy 5:14,4; Romans 12:9–10) Widows, in common with all people, need respect and dignity of self worth. The Lord teaches women to earn honor by being busy in good works and for the family of widows to honor them accordingly and for the church to honor widows indeed. (1 Timothy 5:9–10,4,3)

Women, so live that, if you become bereft of husband and family as an aged widow, you will deserve the honor of being enrolled by the church as a widow indeed. Children and grandchildren, honor your mother and grandmother with the material assistance, love and respect they have earned. Christians, practice pure religion by visiting widows in their affliction. Brethren, "Honor widows who are really widows."

Questions

I. List of Passages Used in This Lesson (Read each passage and be able to discuss its meaning and its application to the lesson.)

Job 24:3	Deuteronomy 26:12-15
Job 31:16-18	Exodus 20:12
Deuteronomy 10:18-19	Deuteronomy 5:16
Deuteronomy 24:17-22	Matthew 15:1-6
Deuteronomy 27:19	Mark 7:5-13
Exodus 22:21-22	Ephesians 6:2-3
Isaiah 10:1-2	Acts 6:1
Isaiah 1:21-23	James 1:27
Isaiah 1:16-17	1 Timothy 5:3-16
Jeremiah 7:5-7	Hebrews 13:2
Zechariah 7:8-14	3 John 5-8
Matthew 23:14	Luke 7:44-46
2 Thessalonians 3:8,10-11	1 Peter 4:9
Genesis 2:15	Matthew 25:35-36
Ruth chapter 2	Acts 9:36-39
1 Kings 17:8-16	Titus 2:3-5
Luke 4:25-26	Romans 12:9-10

II. Terms to Define

1. widow

2. honor

3. really widows (widows indeed)

III. Fact Questions

1. Is widowhood a prospect that most women face?

2. Has there ever been an age in which God did not require those who were able to do so to care for needy widows?

3. What classes of comparatively helpless people did the law of Moses recognize?

4. What responsibilities did Israelites have toward widows?

5. What incentives did God give Israel to fulfill these obligations?

6. What sins did Isaiah charge against Israel concerning widows?

7. How did Judah in Jeremiah's day treat widows? Did God approve?

8. According to Zechariah, how had their treatment of widows contributed to the captivity of the Jews?

9. Did Jesus approve the way the first century Jewish leaders treated widows?

10. What central obligation that children have to their parents was true under the law of Moses and is still true under the law of Christ?

11. Who should provide material assistance to a needy widow who has close relatives?

12. What are the qualifications of those who may be called "really widows" (widows indeed)?

13. Why should younger, impoverished widows not be enrolled to be permanently supported at the expense of the church?

IV. Thought Questions

1. Is it wise to refuse to think about the prospect of becoming a widow or to prepare for that eventuality? (Think: Do you have a life insurance policy on your husband? Why?)

2. Why are widows often comparatively helpless?

3. If we mistreat or ignore the worthy poor, including widows, will God accept our worship and service to Him?

4. Should poor widows who are in good health rely on the help of others without doing any useful work in return?

5. Should we be ashamed to do menial work to provide for ourselves or our family?

6. Why is the ordinance to honor father and mother called the first commandment of the law?

7. How do we honor our parents?

8. Is it right to shift our individual benevolent obligations to the church?

9. Give descriptive titles to each section of 1 Timothy 5:3–16 as divided thus:

    a.   verses 3–8
    b.   verses 9–10
    c.   verses 11–15
    d.   verse 16

10. Are the "really widows" obligated to do work in behalf of the church?

11. Should young women begin to develop the character and do the work that might one day qualify them to be "really widows"? How can they do this?

12. What needs do we all have that widows are often in danger of not having met?

13. How does the Lord provide that each of these needs be met?

IV. Discussion

1. Is it right to put an aged parent in a nursing home?

2. What should young women do to begin to develop the character of "really widows"?

List of Works Cited

Arndt, W.F. and F.W. Gingrich, **A Greek-English Lexicon of the New Testament**.
The Bible, King James Version.
The Bible, New American Standard Bible.
Vine, W.E., **An Expository Dictionary of New Testament Words**.

Lesson Five:

Bible Teachers

Lesson

On the next day we who were Paul's companions departed and came to Caesarea, and entered the house of Philip the evangelist, who was one of the seven, and stayed with him. Now this man had four virgin daughters who prophesied. (Acts 21:8–9)

My introduction to the marvelous light of God's Word goes back in time before my conscious memory to the lap of a godly mother who tenderly taught her son Bible truths and children's hymns. Again, back of my conscious memory is the introduction to preschool Bible classes taught by a woman in the congregation where my father preached in Steele, Missouri. As an adult, I have read and been edified by a number of excellent articles by women. My mother, my wife, and my daughter have engaged me, to my profit, in innumerable discussions of the Scriptures. Women in mixed Bible classes have made comments and asked questions through the years to my immeasurable benefit. As we sang together in public worship and informal gatherings, the beautiful singing of women has edified me countless times. In all these ways and others I, as other men, have properly benefitted from women teachers.

Yet the Scriptures undoubtedly place limitations on the teaching of women in keeping with their divinely assigned role as women.

Let your women keep silent in the churches, for they are not permitted to speak; but they are to be submissive, as the law also says. And if they want to learn something, let them ask their own husbands at home; for it is shameful for women to speak in church. (1 Corinthians 14:34–35)

Let a woman learn in silence with all submission. And I do not permit a woman to teach or to have authority over a man, but to be in silence. (1 Timothy 2:11–12)

This leads us to inquire, What is woman's scriptural role in teaching the Bible?

Women Authorized to Teach the Bible

The New Testament authorizes things in three ways: declaration, approved example, and necessary implication. There are two kinds of declarations: statements and commands. In all these ways, i.e., in every way the New Testament gives the right to act, the Scriptures authorize women to teach the Bible.

> **Authority for Women to Teach the Bible**
> - ★ **Declaration**
>   - ☞ Statement-2 Timothy 2:2
>   - ☞ Command-1 Peter 3:15; Titus 2:3–5
> - ★ **Approved Example-** Acts 18:24–26
> - ★ **Necessary Implication-** Acts 2:17; 21:8–9; 1 Corinthians 11:5; 14:4

The apostle Paul directed Timothy, "And the things that you have heard from me among many witnesses, commit these to faithful men who will be able to teach others also." (2 Timothy 2:2) The word "men" in this passage is a translation of the Greek term *"anthropois,"* which means "universally with reference to the genus or nature, without distinction of sex, a human being, whether male or female." (Thayer. 46) Part of a preacher's work is teaching faithful people, both men and women, to teach the Word of God. Thus, by statement, the apostle authorizes faithful women to teach the Scriptures.

The apostle Peter commands all Christians, men and women, to equip themselves to defend the faith. (1 Peter 3:15) Paul instructs Titus to command aged women to teach practical scriptural truths especially applicable to the feminine gender to young women. (Titus 2:3–5) Thus, women are commanded to teach the Bible.

Priscilla, with her husband Aquila, explained to Apollos, an eloquent preacher who only knew John's baptism, "the way of God more accurately." (Acts 18:24–26) Thus, women are authorized to teach the Word by approved example.

Several passages indicate women received the gift of prophecy. (e.g., Acts 2:17; 21:8–9; 1 Corinthians 11:5) Since the function of a prophet was to teach (1 Corinthians 14:4), it is necessarily implied that women may teach God's Will.

The Scope of Woman's Right to Teach the Scriptures

Women May Teach the Bible
- To Men-2 Kings 22:14–20; Luke 2:36–38; Acts 18:24–26
- In the Assembly-Ephesians 5:19–19
- To Men in the Assembly-Colossians 3:16
- To the Church-Acts 2:17; 21:8–9; 1 Corinthians 11:5; 14:4

Several traditions among some brethren concerning the limitations of a woman's teaching role are without scriptural support. Some brethren to the contrary, a woman may teach a man the will of God. (2 Kings 22:14–20; Luke 2:36–38; Acts 18:24–26) Furthermore, since the command to sing in worship applied to women as well as men, as saints in general and without qualification are taught to sing each to the other, and since we teach when we sing, the Scriptures authorize women to teach in the public worship assembly. (Ephesians 5:18–19) And, since this singing is done when both men and women are present in the worship assembly, women have both the right and obligation to teach men in the assembly. (Colossians 3:16)

In fact, the Scriptures, by necessary implication, authorize women to teach the church. The gift of prophecy was to edify (build up by teaching) the church. (1 Corinthians 14:4) Certain women had the gift of prophecy. (Acts 2:17; 21:8–9; 1 Corinthians 11:5) Therefore, certain women were to edify (build up by teaching) the church. This does not mean a woman should address the whole public worship assembly in the way a preacher does. She could edify the church in some arrangement in harmony with her sphere of life.

But these passages do establish a basic principle. A woman may teach any scriptural truth to anyone, anywhere, in any arrangement, unless there is a Bible restriction prohibiting it.

Scriptural Limitations on Woman's Teaching

> *A woman may teach any Bible truth to anyone, anywhere, in any arrangement, unless there is a Bible restriction prohibiting it.*

Two New Testament passages establish one limitation on the woman's teaching role. The first is 1 Corinthians 14:34–35.

Let your women keep silent in the churches, for they are not permitted to speak; but they are to be submissive, as the law also says. And if they want to learn something, let them ask their own husbands at home; for it is shameful for women to speak in church.

What restrictions do these verses place on women as teachers of the Bible?

This passage is part of a long context in which the inspired writer gives the fullest discussion of miraculous spiritual gifts in inspired literature. (cf. 1 Corinthians 12:1; 13:1; 14:1) In chapter fourteen the apostle regulates the use of these gifts in the public worship assembly. In fact, Paul makes direct reference to spiritual gifts in twenty-one of the forty verses of the chapter. The assembly of First Corinthians chapter fourteen cannot be duplicated today. It is a gross violation of the rules of Bible study to apply the details that regulate supernatural gifts to our assemblies today.

However, the chapter does contain four universal principles that always apply, and the apostle Paul clearly identifies each one. Three times he uses the comprehensive term "all" to point out a permanent truth, and once he states that the principle was true even under the law. These universal principles are:

(1) "Let all things be done for edification." (verse 26)
(2) "God is not the author of confusion but of peace." (verse 33)
(3) Women "are to be submissive." (verse 34)
(4) "Let all things be done decently and in order." (verse 40)

Now look at the passage itself. It is obvious that "churches" in verse 34 and "church" in verse 35 are references to the public worship assemblies of the local church. The immediate context pertains to tongue speakers and prophets addressing the worship assemblies. (verses 27–33)

What were the women to do? The apostle enjoins, "Let your women keep silent in the churches, for they are not permitted to speak." (verse 34) Does this mean no woman may utter a word in the public worship assemblies? If so, women cannot sing (Ephesians 5:19), confess their faith (Romans 10:9–10), or confess sin (James 5:16) in church. The

> **1 Corinthians 14:34–35**
> **Women must not speak in the assembly in such a way that their subjection to man is violated.**

apostle prohibits women from engaging in the kind of speaking of the context—authoritatively addressing the public worship assembly. By doing this women cast off their role of subjection to man. From the very beginning the principle of feminine submission has been true. (verse 35; cf. Genesis 3:16) The lack of subjection demonstrated by the women in Corinth was shameful. The principle is that women must not speak in the assembly in such a way that their subjection to man is violated. Obviously, the principle of this rule would not apply in a church that was composed only of women, as some have been.

The other restrictive passage is 1 Timothy 2:11–12.

Let a woman learn in silence with all submission.
And I do not permit a woman to teach or to have authority over a man, but to be in silence.

The purpose of Paul's first letter to Timothy was to teach him as an evangelist how to conduct himself relative to the church. (1 Timothy 3:14–15) These principles are primarily fulfilled in the local congregation, the only organized relationship divinely authorized for the church.

1 Timothy 2:9–15 gives divine legislation peculiar to godly women and reasons for these commands. Verses nine and ten regulate the dress of women. These requirements apply both in and out of the assembly. Verses eleven and twelve limit the woman in her roles of learning (verse 11) and teaching. (verse 12) Verses thirteen and fourteen state the reasons for the woman's subjection, and verse fifteen assures her she can be saved. These truths do primarily apply to her relationship to the local congregation, in light of the general context, but their application is not limited to the public worship assembly.

Verse eleven regulates a woman's learning. Her activities as a Bible student have two limitations not placed on men: "in silence with all submission."

The term "silence" is from a different Greek word than that used in 1 Corinthians 14:34. It can either mean "*quietness*: descriptive of the life of one who stays at home doing his own work, and does not officiously meddle with the affairs of others" or "*silence*" (Thayer. 281), depending on the context. The **NIV** translates the term as "quietness." The apostle Peter directs women to manifest a "quiet spirit." (1 Peter 3:4) The word "quiet" in 1 Peter 3:4 is a different form of the same word translated "silence" in 1 Timothy 2:11. The principle behind all peculiar limitations on women as students and teachers of the Bible is feminine subjection. In an arrangement, such as a Bible class, where questions and answers are invited, and a man is in charge, a woman may ask a question or offer a comment as long as she is not disruptive or domineering without violating the divine principle of submission. To demand that women not utter a word in congregational Bible study arrangements would contradict the truth that prophetesses could edify the first century church. I conclude that "silence" in 1 Timothy 2:11–12 refers to "quietness," the attitude of one who is not domineering.

> **1 Timothy 2:11–12**
>
> **Women, in their roles as students and teachers of the Bible, must be submissive to men.**

The term "submission" means "a yielding of power or surrendering of person and power to the control of another." (**Webster**. 2277) In short, in all the woman's learning activities in the local church, she must be submissive to male leadership.

Verse twelve limits women as Bible teachers in the local church. It does not forbid women to be teachers over men in secular subjects, such as in college class rooms. Women are forbidden to do two things in the local church in reference to men. They are not to "teach" or "exercise dominion over" men. We have already seen that the Lord authorizes women to teach men, even in the local church. The Scriptures do not contradict themselves. The law of contrast will help us see the apostle's point. Men, in relationship to the church, are to pray everywhere, i.e., in all situations. (1 Timothy 2:8) Paul contrasts the role of women with that of men. (verses 9–15) It should be obvious, since women silently pray with the man who leads, that verse eight refers to men leading in prayer. In contrast, women are not to teach men, i.e., they are not to take the leadership position in teaching men. Nor are women in any other way to "exercise dominion over" men in the local church. The principle is the same as that of 1 Corinthians 14:34–35. Women, in their roles as students and teachers of the Bible in the local church, must be submissive to men.

A Woman Must Not

- Be a Preacher
- Take Any Leading Role in the Worship Assembly When Men Are Present
- Be the Teacher in Charge of a Class Where men Are Present

Practical Application

This limitation on the teaching of women means there are certain things a woman cannot do in expounding the Scriptures. A woman may not be a preacher. Evangelists are to speak "with all authority." (Titus 2:15) This phrase, all of which is translated from the one Greek word "*epitages*," means "with every possible form of authority." (**Thayer**. 244) It is the precise opposite of the phrase "to be submissive" in First Corinthians 14:34, which restricts the woman in her teaching. Literally, the woman in her teaching role, relative to man, must be under authority; whereas the preacher, in his teaching, is to be in authority over. The work of preaching is a role a woman cannot fill.

Furthermore, the fact the woman must be submissive to man in her teaching forbids her to take any leading role in the assembly of the church when men are present. This is the reason the apostle makes special reference to woman's submission when he forbids her to do the kind of speaking some women were doing at Corinth. (1 Corinthians 14:34–35) Everything done in the assembly of the church is to be for edification, i.e., building up by teaching. (verse 26; cf. Hebrews 10:24–25) By taking a leading role in the assembly where men are present, the woman would be teaching over a man. This is the reason women must not make announcements, wait on the Lord's table, lead prayers, lead singing, or take the collection in worship assemblies where men are present.

Additionally, a woman must not be the regularly constituted teacher in charge of a class where men are present. This would place her in the role of exercising dominion over men, in violation of 1 Timothy 2:11–12.

But there are many avenues through which women may properly employ their ability and knowledge as instructors of the divine Word. The most obvious and important task a woman can have in scripture teaching is to instruct her own children in the way of the Lord. (cf. 2 Timothy 1:5; 3:14–15) Since fathers must be gone much of the time to earn a living for their families, who have more opportunity and responsibility to teach God's word to their own children than mothers?

Women may also teach both men and women in arrangements where they are not in authority over men. (Acts 18:24–26) This could simply be in a Bible class of men and women, where a man is in charge, but women are called upon to make comments.

Women certainly are generically authorized to be in charge of classes composed of women or children. (1 Corinthians 11:5; 14:4) Congregations should see that children and women receive the teaching they need by arranging for godly women to teach such classes.

Older women are specifically commanded to teach young women their proper role as women, particularly in the home. (Titus 2:3–5) More congregations should arrange classes for young

Proper Bible Teaching Roles for Women

- Teach Her Own Children
- Make Comments in Mixed Classes of Men and Women
- Teach Over Classes of Women and of Children
- Write Articles

women taught by a godly "mother in Israel." I have known of several instances in which young women desired such instruction, but it was not available.

It is perfectly scriptural for able, knowledgeable women to share their knowledge with both men and women in arrangements in which they are not over men. For example, a column by a respected woman in a gospel paper is very much in order. For years Sister Irene Sowell Foy wrote a wonderful column that did much good in **Preceptor** magazine.

Conclusion

Godly women have a legitimate and important role as teachers of the precious word of God. There is one limitation in principle upon their teaching: a woman may not teach in a position of authority over a man. This is in harmony with her role of subjection based upon her purpose in creation. But there are so many legitimate and important outlets for the ability that women have to teach that there is no excuse for knowledgeable, able women not to be Bible teachers. Churches, use good women in proper capacities to teach the word. Women, use your ability and knowledge, in keeping with your role as a woman, to God's glory, the eternal benefit of the precious children, and the edification of the church.

Questions

I. List of Passages Used in This Lesson (Read each passage and be able to discuss its meaning and its application to the lesson.)

Acts 21:8–9	1 Corinthians 12:1
1 Corinthians 14:34–35	1 Corinthians 13:1
1 Timothy 2:8–15	1 Corinthians 14:1
2 Timothy 2:2	1 Corinthians 14:26
1 Peter 3:15	1 Corinthians 14:27–33
Titus 2:3–5	1 Corinthians 14:40
Acts 18:24–26	Romans 10:9–10
Acts 2:17	Genesis 3:16
1 Corinthians 11:5	1 Timothy 3:14–15
2 Kings 22:14–20	1 Peter 3:4
Luke 2:36–38	Titus 2:15
Acts 18:24–26	Hebrews 10:24–25
Ephesians 5:18–19	2 Timothy 1:5
Colossians 3:16	2 Timothy 3:14–15
1 Corinthians 14:4	

II. Terms to Define

1. men (2 Timothy 2:2)

2. church (1 Corinthians 14:35)

3. silence (1 Timothy 2:11–12)

4. submission

5. with all authority

III. Fact Questions

1. Do the Scriptures place any limitations on the woman in her role as Bible teacher?

2. Are women authorized to be Bible teachers?

3. May a woman teach a man the Bible?

4. May women teach in the public worship assemblies?

5. May women teach men in the public worship assemblies?

6. May women teach the church?

7. Does this mean she should stand before the worship assembly, where both men and women are present, and address the assembly as preachers do?

8. What is the subject of 1 Corinthians chapters 12–14?

9. Is it proper to apply the details of 1 Corinthians chapter 14 to our worship assemblies today?

10. Are there any principles in this chapter which do apply to us? If so, what are they?

11. Does the apostle in 1 Corinthians 14:34–35 forbid women to say anything in the public worship assemblies?

12. What was the overall purpose of Paul's first letter to Timothy?

13. What is the subject of 1 Timothy 2:9–15?

14. What is the specific subject of 1 Timothy 2:11?

15. May women ask questions or make comments in a Bible class composed of both men and women?

16. What is the specific subject of 1 Timothy 2:12?

17. What principle of biblical interpretation helps us to understand the kind of teaching Paul discusses in 1 Timothy 2:11–12?

18. What principle concerning a woman's role as a Bible teacher is taught in 1 Timothy 2:12?

19. May a woman be a preacher?

20. May women take any leading part in the public worship assemblies?

21. May a woman lead or be the teacher over a class composed of both men and women?

22. What Bible teaching roles are open to women?

IV. Thought Questions

1. In what ways does the New Testament authorize us to act?

2. In how many of these ways are women authorized to teach the Bible?

3. When women sing in the worship assemblies, are they teaching?

4. How can we tell what in 1 Corinthians 14 still applies and what does not?

5. Was the principle of feminine subjection different under the law of Moses than it is today?

6. What principle that limits a woman's teaching today is taught in 1 Corinthians 14:34–35?

7. Prove from the Scriptures how the word "silence" is used in 1 Timothy 2:11–12.

8. May a woman teach a college English class with men as students?

9. What general principle concerning a woman's role in the local church is taught in 1 Timothy 2:12?

10. How might a woman violate her feminine role in Bible class discussions?

V. Discussion

   1. If we have a question and answer period after a sermon is preached in the public worship assembly, may women ask questions?

   2. If a congregation were composed only of women, could they conduct worship? Could one of them speak to the assembly? What should they do if a man came into their assembly?

   3. If an American preacher who cannot speak Russian preaches to a Russian congregation, may a woman translate his English into Russian for the audience?

   4. May a woman sign for the deaf in the audience so they can understand a sermon?

List of Works Cited

The Bible, New International Version
Thayer, J.H., **A Greek-English Lexicon of the New Testament**
Webster's Third New International Dictionary, unabridged

Lesson Six:

In the Church

Lesson

Let a woman learn in silence with all submission. And I do not permit a woman to teach or to have authority over a man, but to be in silence. (1 Timothy 2:11–12)

I have been preaching the gospel for thirty-four years. So far as I can recall, every local congregation I have worked with has had more female members than male.

The Lord's church is not immune to the problems of the world. Since the end of World War II, more and more it has become the norm in America for married women to pursue careers outside the home. Now, the ordination of women to the clergy is either accepted by or has become an issue in virtually every denomination. In the Lord's church in the United States, most married women have jobs outside the home. In far liberal churches of Christ women now take leadership roles over men in the worship assemblies. Even in conservative congregations the issue of women participating in decision-making for the church has arisen.

How shall we react to these problems? Shall we go along with the world? Shall we over-react and make laws where God made none? No, of course we must simply find the scriptural answers and follow them. Thus, we inquire, what is the scriptural role of women in the local church?

Limitations on Women in the Local Church

We have already found that feminine subjection to masculine leadership applies in the local church as well as in the home. In both 1 Corinthians 14:34–35 and 1 Timothy 2:11–15, the apostle Paul forbids women to exercise dominion over men.

1 Corinthians 14:34–35 specifically applies this prohibition to the public, worship assembly of the local church, and the over-all context of First Timothy, which qualifies Paul's regulations in 1 Timothy 2:1–15, is direction to the evangelist Timothy on how to "conduct" himself "in the house of God, which is the church of the living God, the pillar and ground of the truth." (1 Timothy 3:14–15) As would be expected, the apostle applies this principle to relationships and activities in the local church, since this is the only organized relationship in the New Testament church.

Thus, there are certain specific activities women must not engage in. As we have already found, women must not take any leadership role in a worship assembly where men are present. Of course, this includes preaching. Nor is it proper for women to be the regularly constituted teachers in charge of classes where men are present. Furthermore, women must not rule over men in the church. (1 Timothy 2:12) To

---

Limitations on Women in the Local church

★ **Principle** ★

Not to Have Authority Over a Man

★ **Applications**

☛ **Must Not Take Leadership Role in Assembly Where Men Are Present**

☛ **Must Not Be a Preacher**

☛ **Must Not Be a Teacher Over Class Where Men Are Present**

☛ **Must Not Participate in Decision-Making for Local Church**

rule is to make decisions that others are obligated to follow. (cf. Exodus 18:21–26) Thus, women must not make or participate in making decisions for the local church, whatever the system is for the decisions to be made, a business meeting or some other expedient arrangement.

Proper Work for Women in the Local Church

Does this mean women are second class citizens in the congregation, to be seen and not heard? Is there nothing women can do to help the local church? To the contrary, there are many things women may scripturally do to help the local church, and several things women may do far better than men.

Women have several obligations to the local church in common with men. They have the responsibilities to faithfully assemble to worship. (Hebrews 10:24–25) They must worship in spirit and truth. (John 4:23–24) When women sing in worship, they are scripturally teaching God's will to all. (Colossians 3:16) What would our worship assemblies be without the beautiful voices of women singing songs of praise and edification? Women must give liberally for the work of the church. (2 Corinthians 9:6–7) Often women, especially widows and wives whose husbands are not Christians, are unable to contribute as much money to the treasury as men, but God is more interested in the attitude that led

Obligations to Local Church Women Have in Common With Men

★ **Worship in Spirit and Truth**

★ **Faithfully Assemble to Worship**

★ **Give Liberally**

★ **Fully Support Each Scriptural Function of Church**

★ **Diligently Do What Work They Are Able and Needed to Do**

★ **Show Love and Concern for Others**

★ **Pray for Others**

to the giving than in the amount of the gift. (Mark 12:41–44) Women, as men, should fully support each scriptural function of the church, such as the Bible classes (James 4:17); diligently do whatever work they are able and needed to do for the church (Romans 12:4–8); show love and concern for each other (Romans 12:9–10,13); and pray for one another. (Ephesians 6:18)

Only the Leadership Roles Are Closed to Women

Thus, in reality, the only areas of service in the congregation closed to women are the leadership roles. A woman who might complain that there is nothing she can do to help the local church is simply looking at the male leadership functions. She needs to learn that greatness in the kingdom is measured by humble service, not the exercise of authority. (Matthew 20:25–28)

But there are several areas of service for which women are generally better qualified than men and which they may scripturally perform, since these activities do not involve being in authority over men. For example, as we have already learned, women may and should teach classes of children and women as a part of the Bible class arrangement of the local church. Surely, molding the minds and character of children is a work of utmost importance demanding knowledge, skill, dedication, and purity of life. Have you ever thought how much the future of the local church depends on the godly women who teach children's classes?

Phoebe, a "sister," was "a servant of the church in Cenchrea." (Romans 16:1) Of her, Paul directed the church in Rome: "...receive her in the Lord in a manner worthy of the saints, and assist her in whatever business she has need of you; for indeed she has been a helper of many and of myself also." (verse 2)

The apostle intimated she had been a helper of many, including himself. This word "helper" (Greek "*prostatis*") is most interesting. W.E. Vine thus explains the word:

> *protectress, patroness;…It is a word of dignity,…and indicates the high esteem with which she was regarded, as one who had been a protectress of many.* **Prostates** *was the title of a citizen of Athens, who had the responsibility of seeing to the welfare of resident aliens who were without civic rights. Among the Jews it signified a wealthy patron of the community.* (Vine. 4:88–89)

Work in the Local Church for Which Women Are Specially Suited

- Teach Classes of Women or Children
- Serve Like Phoebe
- Do Charitable Deeds Like Dorcas
- Practice Hospitality Like Lydia
- Do Good Works Like Widow Indeed
- Give Advice to Men
- Help Select Church Officers
- Help Husbands Become Officers

The apostle does not reveal what her business was, and this means he gives general authority for the church to select a woman or women to serve the church in business that is the scriptural work of the church and does not violate their feminine subjection to male leadership. In fact, he directed the church at Rome to assist her in this work.

Tabitha (Dorcas) is usually remembered because the apostle Peter raised her from the dead. (Acts 9:36–41) But Luke records that she was a "woman full of good works and charitable deeds which she did." (verse 36) When Peter came into the room where her body lay, "all the widows stood by him weeping, showing the tunics and garments which Dorcas had made." (verse 39) Perhaps Tabitha did many other good works, but she obviously made clothing with her own hands to distribute to the poor.

Other areas of benevolent help are identified by the Lord in his description of judgment.

> *Then the King will say to those on His right hand, "Come, you blessed of My Father, inherit the kingdom prepared for you from the foundation of the world: "for I was hungry and you gave Me food; I was thirsty and you gave Me drink; I was a stranger and you took Me in; "I was naked and you clothed Me; I was sick and you visited Me; I was in prison and you came to Me." "Then the righteous will answer Him, saying, "Lord, when did we see You hungry and feed You, or thirsty and give You drink? "When did we see You a stranger and take You in, or naked and clothe You? "Or when did we see You sick, or in prison, and come to You?" "And the King will answer and say to them, "Assuredly, I say to you, inasmuch as you did it to one of the least of these My brethren, you did it to Me." (Matthew 25:34–40)*

Godly women today may accomplish much good by such charitable deeds as making and distributing clothing to needy Christians, cooking for and feeding them, caring for the sick, visiting and caring for those who are shut in by illness and those in nursing homes, and arranging for meals for the family when there has been a death in the congregation.

When Paul and Silas first came to Europe on Paul's second journey of preaching the gospel to the Gentiles, their initial converts were a group of women who worshiped God by the river side at Philippi in Macedonia. (Acts 16:11–15) Immediately after the business woman Lydia was converted to Christ, she begged Paul and his company, saying, "If you have judged me to be faithful to the Lord, come to my house and stay." (verse 15) What a marvelous example of hospitality which godly women should emulate today by receiving traveling preachers and their families into their homes for meals and lodging.

In 1 Timothy 5:9–10 the beloved apostle describes the widows who may be properly supported by the church (They were discussed in full in lesson four).

Do not let a widow under sixty years old be taken into the number, and not unless she has been the wife of one man, well reported for good works: if she has brought up children, if she has lodged strangers, if she has washed the saints' feet, if she has relieved the afflicted, if she has diligently followed every good work.

To qualify, widows had to have practiced hospitality, cared for those in unfortunate circumstances, and diligently performed every good work. Having new members of the church into our homes for meals and visits; helping young, inexperienced, flustered mothers with their children; grading Bible correspondence courses; organizing and keeping track of the books in a church library; doing the same for the church library of sermon tapes; visiting and encouraging the weak and unfaithful; writing letters of welcome to those who visit our worship assemblies; assisting the elders and preacher with secretarial duties, such as typing letters and filing correspondence; addressing a church paper; folding a church bulletin; cleaning the church building; keeping the mailing list current for the church paper; and preparing the communion trays are good works that modern women may do to help the local congregation.

Acts 6:1–6 reveals how the local congregation is to choose its officers. The apostles at this young stage of the church supervised the congregation. (verses 1–2) But in rendering their decision they listened to the members of the church. (Ibid) The "multitude of the disciples" chose the men to serve. (verses 3–6) The method of choosing is not specified. The term "brethren," though masculine, encompasses all the members of the congregation, both male and female. (cf. Romans 12:1 and many other passages) The passage reveals two principles about local church government. The leaders of the church should listen to the advice and opinion of all the members, including the women. In fact, there are some matters of liberty that women usually know much more about than men, such as arrangements and methods for children's classes and interior appearance of the church building and class rooms. For example, in choosing carpeting for a place of worship, why would the elders not actively seek the advice of the women, and perhaps even select an able, devout woman to carry out their decision in buying a carpet and having it installed? The second principle is that all members of the church should have a voice in selecting the bishops to lead and the deacons to serve the church. If a man is placed before the congregation to serve as a bishop, and a woman knows and can document a scriptural reason he is unqualified, should the church refuse to listen to her?

Finally, wives should encourage and assist their husbands so that their husbands will qualify to be elders and deacons in the church. Both elders and deacons must be married men who have the proper rule in their homes. (1 Timothy 3:1–5,12) Their "wives must be reverent, not slanderers, temperate, faithful in all things." (1 Timothy 3:11) Local churches desperately need good men to serve in these offices, and no man ever became a scripturally qualified elder or deacon without the necessary help of a devout and devoted wife.

Conclusion

The Lord designed and prepared woman for the role of helper, primarily in the home, but also in the church. In that role she can accomplish much good to the help of others, the glory of God, and her own salvation. With some reflection, devout women will not ask, Is there anything a woman can do in the congregation? Rather, they will exclaim, How can I find the time to do all I am needed to do?! Godly women, do not seek the leadership role of the man. Devote yourselves to humbly serving the Lord in the church to His glory. Be full of charitable deeds and good works.

Questions

I. List of Passages Used in This Lesson (Read each passage and be able to discuss its meaning and its application to the lesson.)

In the Church • 35

1 Timothy 2:11–15	Ephesians 6:18
1 Corinthians 14:34–35	Matthew 20:25–28
1 Timothy 3:14–15	Romans 16:1–2
Exodus 18:21–26	Acts 9:36–41
Hebrews 10:24–25	Matthew 25:34–40
John 4:23–24	Acts 16:11–15
Colossians 3:16	1 Timothy 5:9–10
2 Corinthians 9:6–7	Acts 6:1–6
Mark 12:41–44	Romans 12:1
James 4:17	1 Timothy 3:1–5
Romans 12:4–10	1 Timothy 3:11–12
Romans 12:13	

II. Term to Define

1. helper

III. Fact Questions

1. What activities are closed to women in the local church?
2. What responsibilities to the local church do men and women have in common?
3. What teaching roles may women fulfill in the congregation?
4. What kind of work did Phoebe do for the church in Cenchrea?
5. What kind of work did Tabitha do?
6. What kinds of good works does Jesus identify by His story of the judgment?
7. What good work did Lydia do?
8. What kinds of works must a woman do to qualify to be really a widow (1 Timothy 5:3–16)?

IV. Thought Questions

1. What is the one principle that limits the woman's role in the local church?
2. If women participate in making decisions for the local church, are they exercising dominion over men?
3. How is greatness in the Lord's kingdom determined?
4. What kinds of work for women does the example of Phoebe authorize?
5. May women help choose the officers of the congregation?
6. How may women help their husbands become elders and deacons?

V. Discussion

1. Should women have any input into the decisions of the local church? Should they be kept informed of decisions made? How may women scripturally offer suggestions for and be informed of congregational decisions?
2. Did Phoebe occupy an office in the local church in the same sense elders and deacons do? (Was she a "deaconess," i.e., a female deacon?)
3. Make a list of works that women may not do in the congregation. Beside it make a list of good works women may do. Which list is longer?
4. Make a list of good works in the congregation you are able to do. Are you doing them? Will you start?

5. Make a list of good works in behalf of the church you could learn to do. Discuss ways to learn how to do them. Will you begin preparing yourself to do these works?

6. Make a list for the men (or elders) of scriptural ways the women of the congregation could be more effectively used.

Work Cited

Vine, W.E., **An Expository Dictionary of New Testament Words**

Lesson Seven:

A Symbol of Authority

Lesson

Now I praise you, brethren, that you remember me in all things and keep the traditions just as I delivered them to you. But I want you to know that the head of every man is Christ, the head of woman is man, and the head of Christ is God. Every man praying or prophesying, having his head covered, dishonors his head. But every woman who prays or prophesies with her head uncovered dishonors her head, for that is one and the same as if her head were shaved. For if a woman is not covered, let her also be shorn. But if it is shameful for a woman to be shorn or shaved, let her be covered. For a man indeed ought not to cover his head, since he is the image and glory of God; but woman is the glory of man. For man is not from woman, but woman from man. Nor was man created for the woman, but woman for the man. For this reason the woman ought to have a symbol of authority on her head, because of the angels. Nevertheless, neither is man independent of woman, nor woman independent of man, in the Lord. For as woman came from man, even so man also comes through woman; but all things are from God. Judge among yourselves. Is it proper for a woman to pray to God with her head uncovered? Does not even nature itself teach you that if a man has long hair, it is a dishonor to him? But if a woman has long hair, it is a glory to her; for her hair is given to her for a covering. But if anyone seems to be contentious, we have no such custom, nor do the churches of God. (1 Corinthians 11:2–16)

When I preached in Nigeria, one of the first questions I encountered was whether or not women are obligated to wear a head covering. In South Africa and Zimbabwe, some women believe they are obligated to wear the head covering in worship, while others do not. In both the Southern and Northern U.S. this question is an emotional one and provokes lively discussion. Is woman obligated to wear an artificial head covering to show her submission?

In First Corinthians 11:2–16 the apostle Paul first praises the Corinthians for following his teaching on the issue he is to discuss. (verse 2) Then he states the universal principles of headship that are true until the end of time. (verse 3) Next he states how the Corinthians were to apply the principle of man's headship over the woman. (verses 4–5) Finally he advanced seven reasons for observing this application. (verses 6–16)

Things NOT in the Text

Things NOT in 1 Corinthians 11:2–16

- **The Public Worship Assembly**
- **Hats or Scarves**
- **Women Wearing Hats or Scarves in the Public Worship Assembly**

Some things many brethren assume to be in this passage are just not there. This passage neither mentions nor implies the public worship assembly. Certainly "praying" and "prophesying" are acts of worship, but a woman could not prophesy in the public worship assembly, since to do so would place her in a position of dominance over men. (1 Corinthians 14:34–35) To "prophesy" was to *"speak forth by divine inspiration."* (Thayer. 553; cf. 1 Corinthians 12:7–11; 14:1) The reasons the apostle Paul advances for a woman to wear a head covering (verses 6–16) apply to women wherever they are, in the public worship assembly or out. The question at Corinth evidently was not whether or not a woman should put on a head covering in worship; it was whether or not she could take off her head covering while praying or prophesying. If women in our society should wear a head covering while praying or prophesying (which no one today can do), they should wear a head covering at all times they are in the presence of men.

Nor does this passage mention hats or scarves. The word "covered" means *"to cover up…to veil or cover one's self."* (Thayer. 331; so Arndt & Gingrich. 412; **ASV**) A hat or scarf is no more a veil than sprinkling or pouring is baptism or playing a piano or organ is singing. In all three instances (head covering, baptism, music in worship) the Lord specified what he wants. Women can no more substitute a hat or scarf for a veil than we can substitute sprinkling for baptism or playing a piano for singing.

Obviously, since the passage neither mentions nor implies the public worship assembly or hats or scarves, women wearing hats or scarves in the public worship assembly is neither mentioned nor implied in the passage.

The Principle

ut I want you to now that the head o every man is hrist, the head o woman is man, and the head o hrist is od.

CHRIST	MAN	GOD
is the head of		
MAN	WOMAN	CHRIST

In verse three the inspired apostle states the principle behind the woman's wearing a head covering. This principle is universal and age lasting. Christ is over man, man is over woman, and God (the Father) is over Christ. These truths apply in all societies, are not changed by culture, and are true until the end of time.

The Cultural Situation

Some facts about Roman society in the first century will help us understand the apostle's message. Greek and Roman women wore a head covering of some sort. "In NT times, however, among both Greeks and Romans, reputable women wore a veil in public…and to appear without it was an act of bravado (or worse)…." (**ISBE**. 3047) However, this custom was not universal among the Jews and was not demanded by the Old Testament, the Jewish Scriptures. "…The use of the veil as a regular article of dress was unknown to the Heb (Jewish—KS) women…. The modern oriental custom of veiling is due to Mohammedan influence…." (Ibid)

Length of the hair was a distinguishing mark between men and women. Roman men, as is depicted on statues and coins, wore their hair short. "…the Jews frequently adopted the fashion of the Romans in cropping the hair closely…." (Ibid. 1320) Women wore their hair long.

Application in Corinth

Every man praying or prophesying, having his head covered, dishonors his head. But every woman who prays or prophesies with her head uncovered dishonors her head, for that is one and the same as if her head were shaved.

Verses four and five apply the principle to the question at Corinth: May women remove their head covering while praying or prophesying? The word "head" is used in two senses in these verses, literally and figuratively. The "head" that is either to be covered or uncovered is the literal head. The one which is honored or dishonored is figurative, meaning "anything *supreme, chief, prominent;* of persons, *master, lord.*" (Thayer. 345)

For a man to wear a head covering as a sign of subjection would be a mark of femininity. It would indicate that he, as the woman, had a head other than Christ. He would thus dishonor his spiritual head, Christ Jesus. The man has only one head, Christ. He must in no way recognize another.

But the woman has a social head upon earth, her husband. And in the local church she must be submissive to the men, giving the men a degree of spiritual headship over women in the congregation (in matters of liberty, i.e., things allowed but not required—1 Corinthians 8:8–9). (1 Corinthians 14:34–35; 1 Timothy 2:11–12) Thus, for her to remove the head covering while praying or prophesying would be an affront to her husband and the men of the congregation.

For her hair to be shaved from her head would be disgraceful, a mark of shamelessness, the sign of an adulteress. But, to put aside the veil and abandon the sign of feminine subjection was just as shameful.

It is important to note that being veiled is not a universal sign in all ages and societies of feminine subjection and chastity. In Canaan in the days of Jacob, a veiled woman sitting beside the road was advertising herself as a prostitute. (Genesis 38:13–15)

Also, it has not always been a shame for a woman to shave her head. The Mosaic law demanded that a Gentile woman captured by an Israelite soldier was to shave her head and mourn her parents for a month before the Israelite could take her to be his wife. (Deuteronomy 21:10–13)

Reasons for This Requirement

In verses six through sixteen the apostle advances seven arguments in favor of women in Corinth retaining their veils while praying or prophesying. All of these arguments support man's role as head and woman's role of subjection. The application to Corinth is that women should wear the veil as a customary sign of feminine submission.

For if a woman is not covered, let her also be shorn. But if it is shameful for a woman to be shorn or shaved, let her be covered. (verse 6)

In Roman society, it was a rejection of feminine subjection for a woman to lay aside her veil. It was equal to having her hair cut short in the manner of men. It was disgraceful, even as shaving her head would be. In Western society, where customarily men wear short hair and women long hair, this principle applies to length of hair. The Lord intends that Christians recognize and follow the cultural distinctions between the sexes of the society in which we live, as long as those customs are not sinful in themselves. Unisex is not a look the Lord accepts.

For a man indeed ought not to cover his head, since he is the image and glory of God; but woman is the glory of man. (verse 7)

Both man and woman were made in the image of God. (Genesis 1:26–27) Mankind is God's glory in that God made us to rule over His creation. (Genesis 1:26,28) But, as the wife is subject to her husband (Genesis 2:18; 3:16), and man's headship over woman is also exercised in the spiritual relationship, the congregation, he is uniquely the glory of God. She is the glory of man, in that she was created in his image. (Genesis 2:18,23)

For man is not from woman, but woman from man. (verse 8)

Man is the head of woman by virtue of the fact that she was created from him, not he from her. (Genesis 2:21–23)

Nor was man created for the woman, but woman for the man. (verse 9)

God did not create man to be woman's helper, but He created woman to be man's helper. (Genesis 2:18)

For this reason the woman ought to have a symbol of authority on her head, because of the angels. (verse 10)

The entire phrase "a symbol of authority" is a translation of one word which literally means simply "authority." Thayer defines the term in this context as *"the power of rule* or *government.* (the power of him whose will and commands must be submitted to by others and obeyed)" (225) He then notes it is in this verse employed to denote *"a sign of the husband's authority over his wife."* (Ibid) In Greek and Roman society the veil was worn by women as a symbol of the authority their husbands exercised over them. To put aside the veil would be an act of rebellion against divinely constituted authority. Angels who rebelliously refused to "keep their proper domain" God "has reserved in everlasting chains under darkness for the judgment of the great day." (Jude 6) This should serve as a warning to women who rebelliously refuse to recognize masculine leadership.

Nevertheless, neither is man independent of woman, nor woman independent of man, in the Lord. For as woman came from man, even so man also comes through woman; but all things are from God. (verses 11–12)

The apostle qualifies his argumentation to limit the man's rule and prevent his arrogance. Nothing he has said should be taken to mean that either woman does not need man or that man does not need woman. It is the Lord's will that the sexes depend upon each other. As he rules her, she helps him. Man is just as dependent upon woman as she is upon him. Yes, woman was created from man. But every man since Adam has come into this world through woman. This exemplifies his dependence upon and need for her. But both man and woman were created by God, are dependent upon him, and must submit to His will. Neither should arrogantly claim independence, whether of existence, need, or will.

Judge among yourselves. Is it proper for a woman to pray to God with her head uncovered? (verse 13)

Their own sense of propriety rooted in their customary ways of demonstrating feminine subjection should demonstrate it was not proper for women to remove their veils while praying.

Does not even nature itself teach you that if a man has long hair, it is a dishonor to him? But if a woman has long hair, it is a glory to her; for her hair is given to her for a covering. (verses 14–15)

Seven Reasons for the Veil

- ★ to be uncovered shameful-verse 6
- ★ woman the glory of man-verse 7
- ★ woman from man-verse 8
- ★ woman for man-verse 9
- ★ because of the angels-verse 10
- ★ to be uncovered not proper-verse 13
- ★ nature-verses 14–15

It will help us apply Paul's lesson if we understand what he means by "nature." The first and literal meaning of the word is *"the regular natural order."* (Arndt & Gingrich. 877) A secondary usage is *"a natural feeling* of decorum, *a native sense* of propriety, e.g. in respect to national customs in which one is born and brought up." (Robinson. 771) Which fits this context? Is short hair on men and long hair on women part of "the regular order of nature"? Do we have an inborn sense that men should wear their hair short and women should have theirs long? Under the law of Moses, a man or woman under the Nazirite vow could not cut their hair. (Numbers 6:2,5) Samson was a Nazirite all his life and was never to cut his hair. (Judges 13:1–7; 16:17) Absalom's extremely long, thick hair was a signal part of his good looks. (2 Samuel 14:25–26) Evidently, "nature" here refers to "*native sense* of propriety" or, as the apostle indicates in verse sixteen, "custom."

Among the Greeks and Romans, it was long established custom, "second nature" so to speak, for men to wear short hair and women long. For a man to have long hair like a woman's was shameful. In our society, where we have the same long established custom, the application to men to wear the hair short is still true. For the woman, however, her long hair, as a sign of feminine subjection, is to her glory. Likewise, the veil, in Corinthian society a symbol of feminine subjection, was to her glory.

But if anyone seems to be contentious, we have no such custom, nor do the churches of God. (verse 16)

Two Greek words are translated "custom" in the King James Version New Testament. One, "*ethos,*" is used of customs demanded by law. (Arndt & Gingrich. 217) This word is used repeatedly of the customs demanded by the law of Moses. (e.g., Acts 6:14; 16:21) This is not the term the apostle employs in 1 Corinthians 11:16. The other word, "*sunetheia,*" found only twice in the New Testament, denotes "*habit, usage.*" (Ibid. 797) It is the word Pilate used in John 18:39, when he inquired of the Jews:

But you have a custom that I should release someone to you at the Passover. Do you therefore want me to release to you the King of the Jews?

This practice was not Jewish law but Jewish habit. The only other New Testament occurrence of this word is in 1 Corinthians 11:16. The apostle did not use the word which refers to law, but the one which refers to habit.

Paul was "a Hebrew of the Hebrews." (Philippians 3:5) The Jews did not have the custom of requiring women to be veiled. The Old Testament made no such requirement. Nor was the custom universal among churches of Christ in the first century. Rather, this was a Greek and Roman custom. If Paul seemed to them to be contentious because he required that women in Corinth be veiled, whereas neither the Jews nor churches of Christ generally followed this practice, it was because the use of the veil was not customary among Jews nor Christians in general.

Modern Application

Two important principles are taught in First Corinthians 11:2–16. The first, upon which the other is based, is the headship of man over woman applicable in the home and the church. The application is that we must follow the innocent customs in the society where we live that distinguish between the sexes and recognize the headship of man.

PRINCIPLES
+ **Man is the head of woman.**
+ **Follow innocent customs of society which distinguish sexes.**

Must women today be veiled? The headship principle of verse three is permanent and universal. But the application of verses four and five is temporary and cultural. The inspired writer specifically calls it a custom in verse sixteen. Thus, the answer to the question depends on the society in which women live. In January, 1992 I was preaching in Ibadan, Nigeria. I was asked if women should wear the head covering. I told them no, because the veil was required in Corinth as a matter of custom. Brother Sunday Ayandare informed me that among the Yoruba tribe, the inhabitants of that part of Nigeria, married women who go in public with bare heads are considered immoral. I apologized to the audience and exhorted the women to wear a head covering in public. Women who live in a society where the head covering is a customary means for a woman to indicate her feminine submission should indeed cover their heads. Women in other societies need not do so. However, a woman whose conscience would be hurt to worship with an uncovered head should cover her head so as not to violate her conscience. Since this is a matter of liberty in societies where the head covering is not a general custom, each woman should do what satisfies her own conscience, but none should bind her conscience on another. (cf. Romans 14:22–23)

Questions

I. List of Passages Used in This Lesson (Read each passage and be able to discuss its meaning and its application to the lesson.)

1 Corinthians 11:2–16	Genesis 3:16
1 Corinthians 14:34–35	Jude 6
1 Corinthians 12:7–11	Numbers 6:2,5
1 Corinthians 14:1	Judges 13:1–7
Deuteronomy 21:12	Judges 16:17
1 Corinthians 8:8–9	2 Samuel 14:25–26
1 Timothy 2:11–12	Acts 6:14
Genesis 38:13–15	Acts 16:21
Deuteronomy 21:10–13	John 18:39
Genesis 1:26–28	Philippians 3:5
Genesis 2:18,21–23	Romans 14:22–23

II. Terms to Define

1. prophesy

2. covered

3. shorn

4. head

5. symbol of authority

6. proper

7. nature

8. custom

III. Fact Questions

1. Does First Corinthians 11:2–16 either mention or imply the public worship assembly?

2. Does the passage mention hats or scarves?

3. Does it mention women wearing hats or scarves in the public worship assembly?

4. What is the principle behind the woman wearing a head covering?

5. What custom prevailed among first century Greeks and Romans pertaining to veils?

6. What custom prevailed concerning differences in hair styles between men and women?

7. Why would a woman have her hair cut short or have it shaved off?

8. How did Paul apply the headship principle at Corinth?

9. What reasons did the inspired writer give the women to cover their heads?

10. Is it God's will that man be independent of woman or that woman be independent of man?

11. Whom do we all depend upon?

12. What are the two great principles of First Corinthians 11:2–16?

A Symbol of Authority • 43

IV. Thought Questions

1. Outline 1 Corinthians 11:2–16
2. What was the question at Corinth which the apostle answers in this passage?
3. Is it all right to substitute a hat or scarf for a veil?
4. Is the principle of First Corinthians 11:3 temporary, local, or cultural?
5. Why did the apostle tell the men at Corinth not to cover their heads?
6. Why did he tell the women they should cover their heads?
7. What is the overall point of the reasons advanced for the women to be veiled?
8. Does this mean the wearing of the veil by women is universally binding?
9. Should women wear their hair in masculine styles?
10. Should men wear their hair in feminine styles?
11. What principle do these requirements exemplify?
12. How is the man God's glory?
13. How is the woman the glory of the man?
14. What is it about angels that showed the women at Corinth they should cover their heads?
15. Is there an inborn sense that long hair is shameful for men but a glory to women?

V. Discussion

1. If the head covering of First Corinthians 11:2–16 is universally binding on women, what does it require women to do?
2. Must women wear a head covering in worship or during prayer?
3. Should all women wear a veil in public?
4. How can you apply these principles to yourself where you live?
5. What should you do if you moved to a society where women customarily wear a veil as a sign of feminine subjection?

List of Works Cited

Arndt, W.F. and F.W. Gingrich, **A Greek-English Lexicon of the New Testament.**
The Bible, American Standard Version.
Farrar, **The Pulpit Commentary.** (volume 19)
International Standard Bible Encyclopaedia.
Robinson, Edward, **Greek and English Lexicon of the New Testament.**
Thayer, J.H., **A Greek-English Lexicon of the New Testament.**

Lesson Eight:

Modest Dress

Lesson

Therefore I desire that the men pray everywhere, lifting up holy hands, without wrath and doubting; in like manner also, that the women adorn themselves in modest apparel, with propriety and moderation, not with braided hair or gold or pearls or costly clothing, but, which is proper for women professing godliness, with good works. (1 Timothy 2:8–10)

Introduction

All right thinking people understand we have a serious problem in our permissive society with indecent dress. All mature Christians realize this problem has invaded the church of the Lord. When I was a boy, I heard Dad lament, "Some women don't wear enough clothing to wad a .22 caliber rifle!" I wonder what he would say now.

God has a standard for our dress that is not dictated by Paris, New York, or Hollywood and does not change with current styles. What is the divine rule for proper clothing?

Modest

Paul instructs, "in like manner also, that the women adorn themselves in modest apparel." The primary meaning of the term "modest" is "orderly, well-arranged." (Vine. 3:79) Thus, some argue that the apostle is simply instructing the women to dress neatly. I cannot comprehend that the Lord would condemn a woman who would wear a baggy, though decent, dress but would exonerate a woman who parades through town in a well-fitting bikini! The simple fact is, He does no such thing. Vine gives a secondary meaning of the term "modest" as "decent," and Thayer notes that in 1 Timothy 2:9 it denotes "decently." (356) Actually, Paul describes modest apparel in the remainder of the passage, and his description is of decent dress, not simply neat clothing.

But what is "decent" dress? Rather than giving a detailed description of such clothing, the inspired writer reveals four criteria of proper dress, each of which pertains to the heart, i.e., to attitudes. To do otherwise would be to limit the application of this portion of the universal gospel to societies in which clothing was identical or essentially parallel to that worn in the first century Roman Empire. But, since Paul addresses himself to attitudes, it is apparent the application is universal.

Thus, the kind of clothing we wear is important because it reflects our hearts. It is also important in that it affects the salvation of others.

With Propriety

Modest dress is "with propriety." The **American Standard Version** correctly renders this "shamefastness." Both Vine (4:17) and Thayer (14) define it as "a sense of shame." Trench explains it to be that sense of shame

which shrinks from overpassing the limits of womanly reserve and modesty, as well as from the dishonour which would justly attach thereto. (71–72)

A woman who dresses "with propriety" is directed by a sense of shame rooted "fast" in her character that prevents her from dressing shamefully.

What, then, is "shameful" dress? Nakedness! (Revelation 3:18) But, who would go naked, other than nudists? Let's see.

When Adam and Eve ate of the tree of knowledge of good and evil, "they knew that they were naked." (Genesis 3:7) They "sewed fig leaves together and made themselves coverings." (Ibid) This term "coverings" means a "girdle, loin-covering." (Gesenius. 292) They had on something like a modern, man's swim suit. When God came walking in the garden, Adam hid, for he was afraid, since he "was naked." (Genesis 3:10) While scantily clothed, the man was still naked, both in his own eyes and in God's. (Genesis 3:11) God "clothed them" by giving them "tunics of skin." (Genesis 3:21) Such garments are "generally with sleeves, to the knees, but seldom to the ancles (sic)." (Wilson. 81) While scantily clothed, the first pair was still naked. That was shameful, immodest. God clothed both the man and the woman with garments that covered them. They were no longer naked. Thus, the Lord revealed a divine standard for decent dress.

This conclusion is confirmed by another Old Testament passage. In a prophecy of Babylon's destruction, Isaiah pictures the ancient city as a "virgin daughter" who would be forced to "Uncover the thigh." Thus, he warns:

"Your nakedness shall be uncovered,
Yes, your shame shall be seen." (Isaiah 47:1–3)

Does this mean one must wear a garment all the way to the knees, completely covering the thigh, to be modest? Not necessarily, although it's not a bad idea, but it certainly indicates that modern swimsuits, see-through clothing, skin-tight clothing, and whatever else indecently exposes the body are shameful.

But "licentiousness" (Galatians 5:19), one of the "works of the flesh" which will bar one from heaven (verses 19–21), is "unbridled lust, excess…outrageousness, shamelessness." (Thayer. 79) This principle applies to men as well as to women. Thus, for a man to dress shamelessly is licentious and sinful. Godly men will not display their scantily clothed bodies before the public either. Men, put on your shirts!

Moderation

The second term descriptive of modest dress is "moderation." Trench explains the term thus:

It is properly the condition of an entire command over the passions and desires, so that they receive no further allowance than that which the law and right reason admit and approve…. that habitual inner self-government, with its constant rein on all the passions and desires. (70,72)

Arndt and Gingrich define the word, *"good judgment, moderation, self control…. Esp. as a feminine virtue decency, chastity."* (810)

Vine simply renders it "sound judgment." (4:44)

The apostle instructs the aged women to teach the younger "to be discreet." (Titus 2:5) This is from the same root as the word "moderation" in 1 Timothy 2:9. Girls and young women, if you want to exhibit sound judgment and decency in your dress, consult with godly, older women in the church. Older women, teach the younger, by both example and word, what such dress is.

Not With Braided Hair or Gold or Pearls or Costly Clothing

The third description of proper dress is negative: "not with braided hair or gold or pearls or costly clothing." Does the inspired apostle forbid women to wear braids in their hair, jewelry, or costly clothing? The "virtuous wife" (Proverbs 31:10) dressed in "fine linen and purple." (Proverbs 31:22) The apostle Peter, in language parallel to Paul's, exhorts women:

Do not let your beauty be that outward adorning of arranging the hair, of wearing gold, or of putting on fine apparel. (1 Peter 3:3)

"Fine" is italicized, an addition of the translators. If we take Simon Peter literally, it is a sin for a woman to put on any clothes! Obviously Peter is using a common Jewish figure of speech, the denial of the lesser to emphasize the greater. (cf. John 6:27) Women of Roman society, as women today, were prone to wear elaborate and expensive hairdos, even to the point of braiding the hair with gold or silver strands or lacing it with gold, silver, or jewels; to dress in outlandish, expensive clothing in order to draw attention to themselves and to their wealth; and to wear expensive jewelry. Sounds like Hollywood, doesn't it? The apostles simply teach women to place the emphasis where it belongs, on

> *the hidden person of the heart, with the incorruptible ornament of a gentle and quiet spirit, which is very precious in the sight of God.* (1 Peter 3:4)

One financially struggling young couple dear to us left a congregation partly because they felt out of place in their drab clothing compared to the expensive clothing and fancy furs sported by others. Some are so conscious of wearing the latest styles with the right labels that they spend exorbitant sums of money, money that could be better used, on unneeded clothing. This excess leads to covetousness (the greedy desire for gain), shames those who cannot afford to so dress, and advertises the vanity of those decked out in such a fashion. Don't place the emphasis on fancy coiffures, designer labels, and costly jewelry that just manifest carnality. Spend your time (and save your money) developing godly character, true inward beauty, which is beautiful to God and godly people and which grows more lovely rather than less so with advancing age. The "hidden person of the heart" doesn't develop wrinkles, age spots, crows feet, and saggy skin!

Proper for Women Professing Godliness

MODEST (DECENT) DRESS
1 Timothy 2:9-10

- ★ **PROPRIETY**
- ★ **MODERATION**
- ★ **NOT WITH BRAIDED HIAR or GOLD or PEARLS or COSTLY CLOTHING**
- ★ **PROPER for WOMEN PROFESSING GODLINESS**

The term "godliness" in 1 Timothy 2:10 is from a term which denotes "the fear or reverence of God." (Vine. 2:162) The Scriptures mention two types of dress for women. Paul admonishes women to wear clothing "which is proper for women professing godliness." Solomon describes the "immoral woman," "the seductress," who wears "the attire of a harlot." (Proverbs 7:5,10) Mary Quant, the London fashion designer who introduced the mini-skirt, brazenly admitted, "Mini-skirts are symbolic of those girls who want to seduce a man." Interestingly, the mini-skirt was introduced in 1964, and the rate of rape rose 90 percent in our country between 1963 and 1968. Do you think there might be a connection? When I was in South Africa, Brother Les Maydell pointed out to me some young women standing by the road dressed in tight fitting, revealing clothing. He said they were prostitutes. Other women were standing nearby waiting for public transportation. They were dressed very modestly in long, loose fitting clothing. At one glance a passerby could tell which were advertising their availability and which were concerned about their reputation. Women, girls, is your clothing "proper for women professing godliness" or "the attire of a harlot"?

Allow me to suggest some questions which should help you answer.

(1) Would you want Christ to see you so dressed? By the way, if you don't want the elders or preacher to see you that way, you ought to know the answer.

(2) Does your clothing cause good men to be tempted to lust? (cf. Matthew 5:27–28; 18:6–7; 2 Samuel 11)

(3) Does the way you dress hinder your influence? (Matthew 5:16)

(4) Could you talk to someone else about immodest clothing dressed the way you are? (Romans 2:21)

Please be honest with yourself in answering these questions.

Conclusion

Christians do not have to dress as the Amish in order to please God. In fact, we are not to show off our religion in our clothing. (Matthew 23:5; Thus, please leave off the shirts with religious messages.) But God does have a standard for our clothing. He wants us to exercise a sense of shame that shrinks from exposing our nakedness; to show sound judgment and decency; to avoid an over emphasis on the outward person shown by gaudy, expensive clothing, hairdos, and jewelry; and to dress in such a way that we exhibit godly character, not immorality. He does not want women or men to tempt the opposite sex to lust by their clothing or lack thereof.

Does your clothing reflect godly character, or does it cause others to stumble and bring shame upon the church? So dress that the reflection of godliness will draw others to Christ.

Questions

I. List of Passages Used in This Lesson (Read each passage and be able to discuss its meaning and its application to the lesson.)

1 Timothy 2:8–10	Proverbs 31:22
Revelation 3:18	1 Peter 3:3–4
Genesis 3:7	Matthew 5:27–28
Genesis 3:10–11	Matthew 18:6–7
Genesis 3:21	2 Samuel 11
Isaiah 47:1–3	Matthew 5:16
Galatians 5:19	Romans 2:21
Titus 2:5	Matthew 23:5
Proverbs 31:10	

II. Terms to Define

1. modest

2. with propriety

3. licentiousness

4. moderation

5. godliness

III. Fact Questions

1. According to the apostle Paul, what are the four criteria of modest dress?

2. Does the Bible give us a specific dress code?

3. What is shameful dress?

4. What are the two kinds of clothing for women mentioned in the Bible?

5. What questions can a woman ask herself concerning her clothing to help her determine if it is modest?

IV. Thought Questions

1. Is it important for a woman to dress modestly? Why?

2. By biblical usage, when is a person naked?

3. Is it necessary for our clothing to come to our knees?

4. Do principles of modest dress also apply to men?

5. What is the best way for girls and young women to learn to use good judgment and decency in their clothing?

6. Is it wrong for women to wear makeup, pretty clothing, pretty hair styles, or jewelry?

7. What principle of dress is the apostle here teaching?

8. Should women place their emphasis on beautiful outward appearance or inward character?

9. Can the way you dress cause others to sin?

10. Should we wear clothing that advertises our religion?

V. Discussion

1. Does the situation affect the standards of modest dress ? For example, is the same clothing appropriate for worship that is proper for playing ball?

2. Does this mean it is proper to wear skimpy or sexually alluring clothing when playing sports or going swimming?

3. Discuss whether or not it is proper:

    a. for teenage girls to be cheer leaders in short skirts.

    b. for teenage girls to wear shorts on a ball team.

    c. for a bride to wear a low cut bridal gown.

4. At what age should we begin teaching our girls to dress modestly?

5. If you can afford to wear more expensive, elegant clothing than other women in the congregation, should you do so?

List of Works Cited

Arndt, F.W. and W.F. Gingrich, **A Greek-English Lexicon of the New Testament**.
Brown-Driver-Briggs-Gesenius, **Hebrew and English Lexicon**.
Thayer, J.H., **A Greek-English Lexicon of the New Testament**.
Trench, R.C., **Synonyms of the New Testament**.
Vine, W.E., **Expository Dictionary of New Testament Words**.
Wilson, William., Old Testament Word Studies

Lesson Nine:

A Virtuous Woman

Lesson

Who can find a virtuous wife?
For her worth is far above rubies.
The heart of her husband safely trusts her;
So he will have no lack of gain.
She does him good and not evil
All the days of her life.
She seeks wool and flax,
And willingly works with her hands.
She is like the merchant ships,
She brings her food from afar.
She also rises while it is yet night,
And provides food for her household,
And a portion for her maidservants.
She considers a field and buys it;
From her profits she plants a vineyard.
She girds herself with strength,
And strengthens her arms.
She perceives that her merchandise is good,
And her lamp does not go out by night.
She stretches out her hands to the distaff,
And her hand holds the spindle.
She extends her hand to the poor,
Yes, she reaches out her hands to the needy.
She is not afraid of snow for her household,
For all her household is clothed with scarlet.
She makes tapestry for herself;
Her clothing is fine linen and purple.
Her husband is known in the gates,
When he sits among the elders of the land.
She makes linen garments and sells them,
And supplies sashes for the merchants.
Strength and honor are her clothing;
She shall rejoice in time to come.
She opens her mouth with wisdom,
And on her tongue is the law of kindness.
She watches over the ways of her household,
And does not eat the bread of idleness.
Her children rise up and call her blessed;
Her husband also, and he praises her:
"Many daughters have done well,
But you excel them all."

*Charm is deceitful and beauty is passing,
But a woman who fears the Lord, she shall be praised.
Give her of the fruit of her hands,
And let her own works praise her in the gates.*
(Proverbs 31:10–31)

Overview

This remarkable description of the ideal wife forms the conclusion to Proverbs, the book of wisdom. It is remarkable for the lofty view it gives of womanhood at a time when women generally were degraded as the property of their husbands or fathers and considered to be fit only for menial labor, even as women are still considered and treated in pagan lands. The thoughtful reader discerns the mind of God in this poem, which elevates woman to the high plain of the divine intention for her stated at creation and restored in Christ. This is not a man's view of womanhood. This is the kind of wife the mother of King Lemuel instructed her son to seek. (Proverbs 31:1)

The twenty-two verses of the text are an acrostic poem; each verse begins with a different letter of the Hebrew alphabet in alphabetical order. The Hebrew alphabet has twenty-two letters, all consonants. The vowels are determined by vowel points beneath the letters. Verse one begins with the Hebrew letter *aleph*, verse two with *beth*, and so on through the alphabet.

Acrostic poems were popular with the Jews, since the Jews placed great emphasis upon memorizing scripture, and the acrostic form made memorizing easier. Proverbs 31:10–31 was meant to be memorized.

Thus, there is no special order to the subject matter in the description of the virtuous wife in verses thirteen through twenty-seven. After we have looked at the poem verse by verse, we will summarize the qualities of ideal womanhood it teaches. Verses eleven and twelve introduce and summarize her character, whereas verses twenty-eight through thirty-one state her reward.

Verse by Verse Comments

(Verse 10, aleph) "Who can find a virtuous wife? For her worth is far above rubies." The word "virtuous" literally means "ability, efficiency." (BDBG. 298) Thus, a footnote in the **Royal Bible, King James Version**, says "virtuous woman" means "Literally *a wife of valor*." There are several statements in the poem which portray either physical or mental strength. For example, "She girds herself with strength" and "She opens her mouth with wisdom." But the word here is used primarily of "moral strength." (Wilson. 469) Thus, when the inspired penman summarizes her "noble character" (**NIV**), he describes her as "a woman who fears the Lord." The virtuous woman, above all else, is a woman of moral strength.

In biblical times men were expected to pay a dowry for a wife (Genesis 34:12; Exodus 22:17; 1 Samuel 18:25), the purchase price of the woman. Thus, women were reduced to property to be bought and sold. This custom still survives, though governments try to eradicate it, in pagan lands. But a virtuous woman is so valuable to her husband that no price can be placed upon her. She is truly priceless, valuable beyond measure. Thus, the mother of Lemuel in one inspired statement destroys the foundation of the custom of purchasing wives, elevates women above the level of a purchased possession, teaches women that their character is more important than their appearance, and teaches her son and all men the kind of wife to look for.

(Verse 11, beth) "The heart of her husband safely trusts her; So he will have no lack of gain." A virtuous woman is completely faithful, so her husband can trust her. Of course, this means she so manages the household affairs that he can trust her not to squander the family money but rather to stretch each dollar. She is to her husband's financial affairs as Joseph, while Potiphar's steward, was to Potiphar's estate. (Genesis 39:1–6) But, even more importantly, she is not like Potiphar's wife, who could not be trusted out of her husband's sight (Genesis 39:7–20), so that by her treacherous lewdness she caused her husband to lose his trusted steward who so effectively managed his affairs. No other factor so undermines the material prosperity of a family, as well as its spiritual strength, as sexual unfaithfulness. It leads to the destruction of families and causes the financial and spiritual ruin of those involved. The virtuous woman is the opposite of the crafty woman who brings the destruction of all who follow her. (Proverbs chapter 7) In contrast to the virtuous woman, the crafty woman is "immoral" (7:5), attired as an harlot (7:10), "loud and rebellious" (7:11), faithless to her husband (7:18–20) and enticing in speech. (7:21) She brings ruin and death to all who trust her (7:22–27) and is in reality foolish. (9:13–18)

(Verse 12, gimel) "She does him good and not evil All the days of her life." A good figure and a beautiful face are fleeting and empty of real value, but the trustworthiness of noble character cause life long good and no harm to her husband. In fulfillment of her wedding vows, she is his most dependable earthly helper in wealth or poverty, in health or illness, in good times or bad, in the vigor of youth and in the frailty of old age.

(Verse 13, daleth) "She seeks wool and flax, And willingly works with her hands." In the ancient Near East women of the household made all the clothing for the family. Wool and flax were two chief fibers used in making cloth. Flax was the raw ingredient for manufacturing linen. She did not have to be pressed into providing clothing for her family. She sought the material and willingly worked to make clothing for her family.

(Verse 14, he) "She is like the merchant ships, She brings her food from afar." Merchant ships ranged far and wide around the Mediterranean world and down the Red Sea bringing the best products. Even so, the virtuous woman traveled from shop to shop to find the best in food buys for her family. Today, the frugal house wife in Nigeria goes from stall to stall in the market to find the best food stuffs at the lowest prices; and her sister in America looks through the sales advertisements, clips coupons, compares prices, and looks at the supermarket for the freshest, most nutritious, least expensive food items for the good of her family.

(Verse 15, waw) "She also rises while it is yet night, And provides food for her household, And a portion for her maidservants." This is the picture of the mistress of a wealthy household. Remember, these are the thoughts of a queen mother. But the principle applies in the humblest of households. In her diligence to manage household affairs she rises early, before the rest of the house, to see that all the family receives a nutritious breakfast and that the workday is planned for her helpers. In modern Africa this would be her daughters, and American mothers should so direct the household chores for their daughters.

(Verse 16, zayin) "She considers a field and buys it; From her profits she plants a vineyard." By her prudent management of the household budget she is able to save to buy a field in which to plant a vineyard. Here she labors to produce the crop that will further increase the family finances. She is engaging in work outside the home that, rather than interfering with her homemaking, supplements the family income. She is a wise manager, shrewd business person, and hard worker.

(Verse 17, heth) "She girds herself with strength, And strengthens her arms." The ancients would bind up their outer wear, the long, flowing robe, with a sash when working, to keep it out of the way. They were thus prepared to toil without interference. The strength that comes from hard, physical toil is her preparation. She is ready to work. The virtuous woman is not a soft, dainty thing unwilling to dirty her hands and exert her muscles in laborious toil for her family.

(Verse 18, teth) "She perceives that her merchandise is good, And her lamp does not go out by night." She is not satisfied with shoddy goods. The articles she makes for sale are well made and deserve a premium price. She works into the night to accomplish her tasks. Perhaps this is the basis for the old saw, "Man works from sun to sun, but woman's work is never done."

(Verse 19, yod) "She stretches out her hands to the distaff, And her hand holds the spindle." The distaff and spindle were tools for spinning thread.

Usually, the distaff, containing the loosely wound flax or wool fiber, is held in the crook of the left elbow, as the left hand guides the fiber that is being spun into a string or cord leading to the spindle, as the spindle is rotated in the right hand. To skillfully manipulate both the distaff and spindle required a great amount of practice and dexterity on the part of the lady. The term "distaff" ultimately became the term used for women's work in general. (Martin. 5)

She is busily and skillfully preparing clothing for her family.

(Verse 20, kaph) "She extends her hand to the poor, Yes, she reaches out her hands to the needy." "This godly woman is not selfish; not only caring for her own family and household, but she is aware of the needy. She shows mercy and charity toward those in need outside her family." (Ibid. 6) She is a Dorcas. (Acts 9:36) Her work is done not just to increase family wealth but to help the worthy poor. (Acts 20:35; Ephesians 4:28)

(Verse 21, lamed) "She is not afraid of snow for her household, For all her household is clothed with scarlet." Scarlet dye was made from a worm and characteristically used on wool. The dark color and heavy fabric held in the body heat. Thus, she did not fear winter or other difficult times, because she wisely, diligently prepared her family for those situations that were sure to arise.

(Verse 22, mem) "She makes tapestry for herself; Her clothing is fine linen and purple." "Tapestry" probably refers to decorative bed coverings or decorative pillows. "Purple" was the expensive clothing worn by the wealthy and royalty, dyed with a deep purple dye made from a shell fish. She is able to wear pretty clothing and decorate her house tastefully because she is frugal, hardworking, skillful in management, and makes her own fabrics. This is not a license for women to decorate lavishly or to concentrate their thoughts, time, and money on expensive clothing (1 Peter 3:3–4), but it states the material reward of virtuous character.

(Verse 23, nun) "Her husband is known in the gates, When he sits among the elders of the land." The rule of the older men was rooted in the patriarchal age. The law of Moses made provision for the custom of the older heads of houses to judge civic affairs. (cf. Deuteronomy 22:13–18) Ancient cities were walled with narrow streets. City business was conducted in the one broad, open area in town where all commerce took place, inside the city gates. To sit among the elders was to be honored as a town father who with other elders passed judgment in both public and private disputes. From this honored position came the elders of the synagogue and eventually the elders of the church. The virtuous wife so managed the household affairs, both material and spiritual, that her husband was honored as an elder of the city. So today, no man ever became a qualified elder of the church without the help of a virtuous wife. (1 Timothy 3:11) She is "the crown of her husband." (Proverbs 12:4)

(Verse 24, samek) "She makes linen garments and sells them, And supplies sashes for the merchants." Through her hard, long toil, she not only provided the clothing for her own family but even had surplus to sell to merchants. She could trade with the merchants for the purple for her own clothing. She operated a "cottage industry."

(Verse 25, ayin) "Strength and honor are her clothing; She shall rejoice in time to come." People are often known and judged by the clothing they wear, and most place great emphasis on clothing. That by which she is known and upon which she places emphasis are strength and honor. "She is invested with a moral force and dignity which arm her against care and worry." (Deane. 601) She is prepared for the future, both here and hereafter.

(Verse 26, pe) "She opens her mouth with wisdom, And on her tongue is the law of kindness." Her speech reveals the wisdom and godliness of her mind. (Matthew 12:34–35) Her speech is not characterized by gossip, filth, taking the Lord's name in vain, or even worldly affairs. Rather, she speaks words of wise guidance and kindness to her household.

(Verse 27, tsadde) "She watches over the ways of her household, And does not eat the bread of idleness." She is a wise household manager and a hard worker.

(Verse 28, qoph) "Her children rise up and call her blessed; Her husband also, and he praises her:" What is the reward of such a woman? The one she values the most is the grateful appreciation of her own family. What can lift her spirit more than to hear her child honestly say, "Mommy, you're the best mommy in the world." What can make her feel more valuable than to hear her husband truthfully declare, "Honey, no man could ask for a better wife." Husbands and children should appreciate and demonstrate their appreciation for such an excellent wife and mother.

(Verse 29, resh) "'Many daughters have done well, But you excel them all.'" The term "well" is the adverb form of "virtuous." (cf. KJV) "This woman is described as being equal to the very best. To "do virtuously" means that she had acted with force and strength of character and in a beneficial manner for others." (Martin. 7) This is what her family says to her with honesty.

(Verse 30, shin) "Charm is deceitful and beauty is passing, But a woman who fears the Lord, she shall be praised." In the poetic parallel, "charm" probably refers to "loveliness of form" (Deane. 602), i.e., a good figure, whereas "beauty" describes a pretty face. Outward beauty is deceptive in that it often masks a hideous character, and is passing in that it fades with the advance of age. Far more deserving of praise is the woman who fears the Lord, i.e., the virtuous woman, than the physically beautiful woman.

(Verse 31, tau) "Give her of the fruit of her hands, And let her own works praise her in the gates." This woman receives just praise from her family and all who know her. The prosperity and honor which are hers are the just reward for sacrificial labor, which is in turn the proof of godly character.

Summary

A virtuous woman, one who truly fears the Lord and has the moral strength that reflects it, is valuable beyond price to her husband and family. She is completely trustworthy, works long hours willingly for her family, wisely manages the household affairs, increases the family wealth by spending wisely and supplementing her husband's income, is kind to the needy, prepares her family for difficult times, and employs speech that guides her family into wisdom and kindness. She is a source of spiritual strength to her husband and children, and causes her husband to be respected and honored as well. Such a woman will characteristically and justly enjoy security and prosperity. She receives the sincere praise of her husband, children, and acquaintances. Truly, she is priceless.

Questions

I. List of Passages Used in This Lesson (Read each passage and be able to discuss its meaning and its application to the lesson.)

Proverbs 31:10–31	Acts 9:36
Proverbs 31:1	Acts 20:35
Genesis 34:12	Ephesians 4:28
Exodus 22:17	1 Peter 3:3–4
1 Samuel 18:25	Deuteronomy 22:13–18
Genesis 39:1–20	1 Timothy 3:11
Proverbs chapter 7	Proverbs 12:4
Proverbs 9:13–18	Matthew 12:34–35

II. Terms to Define

   1. acrostic

   2. virtuous

   3. dowry

   4. distaff

   5. spindle

   6. tapestry

   7. purple

   8. well

   9. Charm

III. Fact Questions

   1. Who is the author of Proverbs 31:10–31?

   2. What kind of literature is this passage?

   3. What are the three sections of this poem?

   4. Explain the immediate meaning to those of King Lemuel's day of each verse of the poem.

IV. Thought Questions

   1. Why did the Hebrews write acrostic poems?

   2. How valuable is a virtuous woman?

   3. In what ways is the virtuous woman trustworthy?

   4. How lasting is the value of a virtuous woman to her husband?

   5. What applications can you make from each verse to women today?

   6. What are the rewards in this life to a woman who is virtuous?

V. Discussion

   1. How does the picture of the virtuous woman of Proverbs contrast with:

      a. the general view in ancient times?

      b. the view in pagan lands today?

      c. the view in Moslem countries?

      d. the ideals of the women's liberation movement?

      e. the views of people, both men and women, with whom you associate?

   2. Should women today try to duplicate every specific activity of the virtuous woman of Proverbs?

   3. What qualities of character does she exemplify that women should strive to have?

   4. In what areas could you improve your life to do this?

   5. How could you use this passage to:

      a. train your daughters?

b. train your sons?

c. teach your sons the kind of wife they should seek?

List of Works Cited

The Bible, King James Version.
The Bible, New International Version.
Brown-Driver-Briggs-Gesenius, **Hebrew and English Lexicon.**
Deane, W.J., **The Pulpit Commentary.** Volume 9.
Martin, Luther W., "The Words of King Lemuel as Taught By His Mother—Proverbs 31:10–31," **Faith and Facts** Quarterly. Volume 24, Number 1. (January, 1996)
Wilson, William. **Old Testament Word Studies.**

Lesson Ten:

Unfading Beauty

Lesson

Your beauty should not come from outward adornment, such as braided hair and the wearing of gold jewelry and fine clothes. Instead, it should be that of your inner self, the unfading beauty of a gentle and quiet spirit, which is of great worth in God's sight.
(1 Peter 3:3–4, **New International Version**)

In 1995 American women sank 81.7 billion dollars into visits to beauty shops. (**Statistical Abstract**. 778) In addition, they bought cosmetics, creams, perfumes, colognes, hair spray, and nail polish. Purchases were made of products guaranteed to shrink cellulite, remove wrinkles, change the color of skin (tan or bleach), eliminate age spots, straighten or curl hair, and color hair. And this is not to mention expensive jewelry and elegant clothing. Some women literally spend hours before a mirror before they will go out in public.

And to what end? For those who have the money and the skill, the outward person is temporarily more beautiful—unless sun, wind, or rain brings a quick end to the laboriously wrought loveliness. Regardless, even for those who diet, exercise, rest, and care for their skin and hair, time is the unyielding ravager. The Hollywood beauties of yesteryear simply display their vanity when they attempt to appear to be sexually alluring.

There is a beauty which appeals far more to godly men and women, the only beauty the Lord will notice. It is a beauty which time enriches rather than ravages. It costs nothing. It is equally available to a peasant from the African bush or a college beauty queen (Actually, the beauty queen is at a severe disadvantage). It is a beauty which never leads to fornication but always forms the basis of a joyful, lifetime marriage. It never brings a leering stare of lust or wolf whistle from a slob who views you as a sex object but often causes admiration and love to swell in the breast of a righteous young man looking for a worthy lifelong companion. It is the unfading beauty of a righteous character. In this lesson we will study three New Testament passages which reveal the splendid jewels of character which adorn the inward beauty of a godly woman.

1 Timothy 2:15
Nevertheless she will be saved in childbearing if they continue in faith, love, and holiness, with self-control.

In 1 Timothy 2:9–15 the apostle Paul speaks of the proper role of women in relation to the local congregation. They must maintain their feminine subjection. But women are heirs of salvation with men, so long as they maintain their feminine role (summarized by the term "childbearing"). But to be saved, women, as men, must maintain four qualities—"faith, love, and holiness, with self-control."

Faith

The term "faith" means "trust, confidence, conviction, firm persuasion." Saving faith is defined by inspiration: "Now faith is the substance of things hoped for, the evidence of things not seen." (Hebrews 11:1) The **New American**

Standard Bible translates this verse, "Now faith is the assurance of things hoped for the conviction of things not seen." Faith, in relationship to hope, is assurance. It stands under and supports our hope. Thus, our hope is no more secure than our faith is strong. Saving faith is conviction about unseen things based on evidence. It is not blind acceptance of unprovable opinions, nor is it based on emotion.

Faith is absolutely essential to our salvation. (Hebrews 11:6) Furthermore, it is the principle which guides the Christian's life. "For we walk by faith, not by sight." (2 Corinthians 5:7) It is absolutely a waste of time to reason with women about their proper role in the home and in the church until they have faith. Why should an infidel listen to the apostle Paul, when she perceives him to be a woman hating old bachelor? But the reason many women who claim to be Christians ignore biblical teaching on the home and the church is their lack of faith. It takes great faith for a woman to submit to an unbelieving husband who is selfish and cruel in his demands. It takes faith for a young woman with a college degree to stay at home and care for her children, when she must do without the finer house and car as well as the prestige she could have as a "career woman."

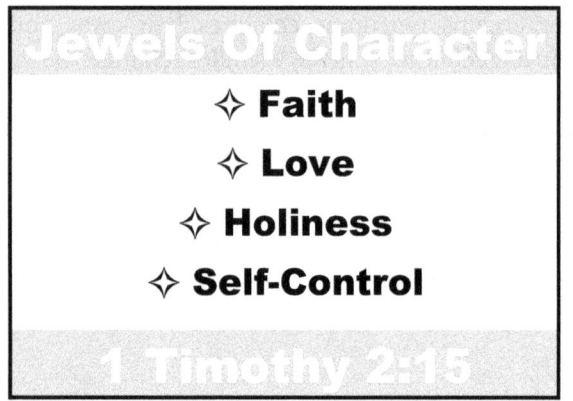

Love

Surely no English word is more misused and no Scripture concept more misunderstood than love. The love that forms the crowning attribute of the Christian's character is not an emotion. You may not feel like hugging a woman who has spread malicious gossip about you, but you must love her. (Matthew 5:43–44) Love does not mean we ignore sin. Jesus loved His fleshly people the Jews intensely, but He denounced their sins scathingly. (Matthew 23:33,37) Rather, love is active good will. (1 John 3:16–18) It is doing what is best for the object of love. It is the highest quality of our character (1 Corinthians 13:13; Colossians 3:14), the attribute in which we most nearly approach the moral nature of God (1 John 4:8), and must be the motive for every act of our lives. (1 Corinthians 16:14)

Holiness

The primary meaning of "holiness" is "separation to God" (Vine. 2:225), and this term is used of "the conduct befitting those so separated." (Ibid; cf. 1 Thessalonians 4:7) It is also translated "sanctification." (cf. 1 Thessalonians 4:3–4) God is holy, and our conduct should reflect His holiness. (1 Peter 1:15–16) We exercise holiness by maintaining purity from sin. (2 Corinthians 7:1) We cannot be saved without doing this. (Hebrews 12:14)

Self-control

This is the word translated "sobriety" in the **King James Version** and is derived from the term translated "discreet" in Titus 2:5. It primarily means *"of sound mind, sane, in one's senses."* (Thayer. 613) When Festus accused Paul of insanity, the apostle replied, "I am not mad, most noble Festus, but speak the words of truth and reason." (Acts 26:25) The word "reason" is this same term in the original Greek. But, as a manifestation of soundness of mind, the word secondarily means *"curbing one's desires and impulses, self-controlled, temperate."* (Thayer. 613) R.C. Trench well describes the word as here used:

> *It is properly the condition of an entire command over the passions and desires, so that they receive no further allowance than that which the law and right reason admit and approve...that habitual inner self-government, with its constant rein on all the passions and desires.* (70,71)

The apostle Paul most emphatically did not look down on women. He expected them to exercise the same soundness of mind he claimed for himself and to reflect that sound mind by exercising the self-control that reins in bodily passions and does not allow them to be fulfilled in unlawful ways. He condemned, "gullible women loaded down with sins, led away by various lusts." (2 Timothy 3:6) He expected women to have the good sense not to fall for the smooth flattery, vain promises, and good looks of a seducer.

Titus 2:3–5
The older women likewise, that they be reverent in behavior, not slanderers, not given to much wine, teachers of good things— that they admonish the young women to love their husbands, to love their children, to be discreet, chaste, homemakers, good, obedient to their own husbands, that the word of God may not be blasphemed.

In fulfilling his obligation to "speak the things which are proper for sound doctrine," Titus was to both instruct older women how to behave and teach them what to teach the young women. The apostle both revealed traits that pertained to older women and that the older women were to instruct the young women to follow.

Reverent in Behavior

This is the only occurrence of the word translated "reverent" in the Bible. It is a compound term, which primarily means "that which corresponds to…the temple precincts and ministry." (**TDNT**. 3:253) The use of this term is a reminder to older women to "take seriously the fact that" they "belong to God." (Ibid. 54) Older women, younger women who are trying to live for Christ look up to you as examples, as they indeed should. Never forget, in any situation, that you belong to God.

Not Slanderers

This is the word translated "devil" and means "false accuser." (Thayer. 135) When a woman's children are grown and no longer demand her constant attention, she may have extra time on her hands. (cf. 1 Timothy 5:13) It is easy to become a busybody, picking up scraps of dirty information, some true, some false, that injure the reputation of others. The devil deals in such slander. (cf. Job 1:8–11; 2:3–5)

When one traffics in verbal garbage, repeating filthy pieces of damaging tales about others, she is acting like the devil himself. Gossip brings trouble on the gossiper (Proverbs 21:23), stirs up strife (Proverbs 26:20–21), and hurts the one gossiped about. (Proverbs 26:22) God hates gossip! (Proverbs 6:16–19) Before you repeat anything about another person, ask yourself four questions. Is it true? (Are you sure?) (Ephesians 4:25) Will it do any good to tell it? (Ephesians 4:29) Will it help everyone involved to tell it? (Ibid) Have you spoken to the person you are speaking about concerning the matter? (Galatians 6:1)

Not Given To Much Wine

The **American Standard Version** translates this clause "nor enslaved to much wine." The **New International Version** has the word "addicted." The term rendered "given," "enslaved," or "addicted," literally means to *"become a slave to someone."* (Arndt & Gingrich. 205) The apostle is instructing Titus to warn older women against becoming addicted to wine. Be careful not to view the prohibition against enslavement as an implied approval of moderate use. The apostle Peter warns against "excess of riot." (1 Peter 4:4, **KJV**, "flood of dissipation," **NKJV**) Is a little riot (dissipation) all right? The passage is a warning against a specific misuse of wine, not a tacit approval of wine. The Bible uniformly warns about the use of alcoholic beverages (e.g., Proverbs 23:29–35), and the New Testament specifically forbids both drunkenness and social drinking. (1 Peter 4:3–5) The only use of alcoholic wine sanctioned by the New Testament is medicinal. (1 Timothy 5:23) Because of ailments common to and unique to them, older women have a tendency to depend more on medicine. It is certainly good to take specific medicines for specific health problems, but we should carefully avoid addiction to pain killers, tranquilizers, or other enslaving drugs.

Teachers Of Good Things

With their increased spare time and the knowledge and wisdom gained by years of study and experience, rather than spending the time and using the tongue to trade in gossip, older women should be teachers of the young women. This, of course, implies that younger women should be willing to listen to the advice and look to the example of older, godly women. Indeed, young women should be anxious to receive the instruction of the righteous older women, for this is the best way for them to learn the practical application of the gospel to their lives as women and to learn how to fulfill in a way pleasing to God their roles in the home. The term "admonish," used of what the older women do as teachers, is from the same word family as the term "self-control" in 1 Timothy 2:15 and "discreet" in verse five. It primarily means *"to restore one to his senses"* and then *"to exhort earnestly."* (Thayer. 613)

> **Jewels Of Character**
> ⬥ Reverent in Behavior
> ⬥ Not Slanderers
> ⬥ Not Given to Much Wine
> ⬥ Teachers of Good Things
> ⬥ Discreet
> ⬥ Chaste
> ⬥ Good
> **Titus 2:3–5**

Discreet

This is the same idea as "self-control" in 1 Timothy 2:15.

Chaste

This is a close synonym of the word "holiness" in 1 Timothy 2:15 and has the exact application of being "pure and undefiled." (Trench. 334) Paul told the Corinthians, "For I am jealous for you with godly jealousy. For I have betrothed you to one husband, that I may present you as a chaste virgin to Christ." (2 Corinthians 11:2)

Good

Vine says this word "describes that which, being good in its character or constitution, is beneficial in its effect." (2:163) "Applied to persons, it signifies the excellence of the person in his existing position." (**TDNT**. 1:10) Young women should learn from older women how to be good wives, good mothers, and good in all their peculiar roles as women.

1 Peter 3:1–4

Wives, likewise, be submissive to your own husbands, that even if some do not obey the word, they, without a word, may be won by the conduct of their wives, when they observe your chaste conduct accompanied by fear. Do not let your adornment be merely outward—arranging the hair, wearing gold, or putting on fine apparel— rather let it be the hidden person of the heart, with the incorruptible beauty of a gentle and quiet spirit, which is very precious in the sight of God.

Gentle

This is the word which is also translated "meekness." It was a fundamental trait manifested by Jesus (Matthew 11:29), one of the eight qualities which are to distinguish citizens of the kingdom of heaven (Matthew 5:5), and an essential element of true wisdom. (James 3:17) Worldly people, by inclination and training selfish and self-assertive, view meekness as weakness. But true gentleness or meekness is a great quality of character reflective of true inner strength and necessary to salvation. The word is primarily "used of animals which have been tamed, and which have learned to accept discipline and control." (Barclay. 113–14) My dog Dixie, who would fetch a stick or a newspaper, shake hands, sit, and come when called, was a gentle (meek) pet. Gentleness is first and foremost "towards God.

It is that temper of spirit in which we accept His dealings with us as good, and therefore without disputing or resisting." (Vine. 3:55) Thus, a gentle woman is submissive to God's will and does not try to rebel against it. (James 1:21)

This meekness, however, being first of all a meekness before God, is also such in the face of men, even of evil men, out of a sense that these, with the insults and injuries which they may inflict, are permitted and employed by Him for the chastening and purifying of His elect. (Vine. 56)

Therefore, a meek woman is gentle to other people, even to an unbelieving husband who hurls curses and insults at her and heaps abusive treatment upon her. (cf. 1 Thessalonians 2:7; Titus 3:1–2)

Described negatively, meekness is the opposite to self-assertiveness and self-interest; it is the equanimity of spirit that is neither elated nor cast down, simply because it is not occupied with self at all. (Vine. 56)

Through the crucifying of self, the meek woman has gained an inner mastery of her emotions, so she is neither in the depths of depression nor inflated with self importance. Thus, gentleness (meekness) is submission to God, gentleness to other people, and control of one's inner self. It is true strength of character.

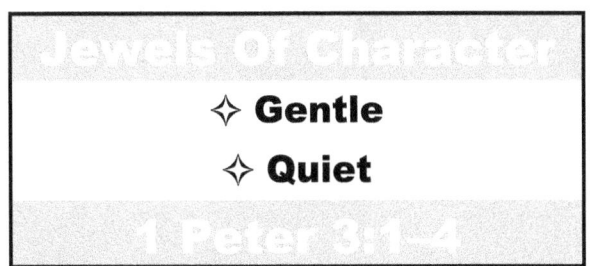

Jewels Of Character
✧ **Gentle**
✧ **Quiet**
1 Peter 3:1–4

Quiet

"Quietness" denotes "tranquillity arising from within, causing no disturbance to others." (Vine. 3:242) A quiet woman is the opposite of the busybody who spends her time meddling in others' affairs. (2 Thessalonians 3:11–12) "A tranquillity of heart reflects a tranquillity in behavior." (Hamilton. 131) Godly women mind their own business and do not stick their noses into the affairs of others.

Conclusion

For those women who seek a loveliness that is more than skin deep, that appeals to godly people of both sexes, that costs nothing, that grows more beautiful with advancing age, and that alone appeals to the Lord, there is a beauty of inestimable value that can be yours. It is a beauty that even lasts beyond the grave and remains eternally. It is a loveliness available to the poor, despised, and unfavored in face and figure as well as to the wealthy, famous and lovely of appearance and form. It is a loveliness that, though it will not gain you fame, fortune or popularity, will bring you eternal peace and joy. It is the unfading beauty of godly character, "which is very precious in the sight of God." Spend a lifetime developing this beauty, and it will bring you an eternity of bliss.

Questions

I. List of Passages Used in This Lesson (Read each passage and be able to discuss its meaning and its application to the lesson.)

1 Timothy 2:9–15	Job 1:8–11
Hebrews 11:1	Job 2:3–5
Hebrews 11:6	Proverbs 21:23
2 Corinthians 5:7	Proverbs 26:20–22
Matthew 5:43–44	Proverbs 6:16–19
Matthew 23:33,37	Ephesians 4:25
1 John 3:16–18	Ephesians 4:29
1 Corinthians 13:13	Galatians 6:1
Colossians 3:14	Proverbs 23:29–35

1 John 4:8
1 Corinthians 16:14
1 Thessalonians 4:7
1 Thessalonians 4:3–4
1 Peter 1:15–16
2 Corinthians 7:1

1 Peter 4:3–5
1 Timothy 5:23
2 Corinthians 11:2
1 Peter 3:1–4
Matthew 11:29
Matthew 5:5

II. Terms to Define

1. faith
2. love
3. holiness
4. self-control
5. reverent
6. slanderers
7. given
8. admonish
9. discreet
10. chaste
11. good
12. gentle
13. quiet

III. Fact Questions

1. What kind of beauty should women concentrate on?
2. How does the Bible define saving faith?
3. What is the relationship between faith and hope?
4. What is the relationship of faith to evidence?
5. How does faith relate to the unseen things of God?
6. Are our opinions, unsupported by Scripture, properly called "faith"?
7. Can we be saved without faith?
8. How important is faith in our daily lives as Christians?
9. Should we love even our enemies?
10. How crucial is love as a quality of our character?
11. Can we be saved without being holy in life?
12. How do we exercise holiness?
13. How do we manifest self-control?
14. To whom do we belong as Christians?
15. What moral danger do older women face as they have the luxury of extra time on their hands?
16. Who is the ultimate example of a slanderer?
17. What danger in relationship to medicine do many older women face?
18. How do women exhibit quietness?

IV. Thought Questions

1. Does it do any good to argue about the scriptural role of women with someone who doesn't believe the Bible?

2. What is the fundamental reason many women who call themselves Christians ignore their God-ordained roles as women?

3. If we love others, do we overlook their sins?

4. What quality of the Christian's character is most like God's moral nature?

5. Did the apostle Paul look down on women?

6. What obligations do older women and young women have to each other?

7. What are the dangers of gossip?

8. What questions should you ask yourself before you repeat something you heard about another person?

9. Does the prohibition against addiction to wine mean moderate drinking of alcoholic beverages is approved?

10. Does the Bible give its approval to drinking alcoholic beverages for pleasure or to socialize?

11. What use of alcoholic beverages does the New Testament approve?

12. What principle concerning the use of medicine do we learn from the command not to be addicted to wine?

13. How important is gentleness to our character?

14. How is gentleness expressed in relationship to:

   a. God?

   b. other people?

   c. our own emotions?

15. Is gentleness indicative of strength or weakness?

V. Discussion

   1. Is it wrong for women to wear makeup, jewelry, and stylish clothing and to have stylish hair dos?

   2. How can you go about incorporating these jewels of a beautiful character into your life?

List of Works Cited

Arndt, W.F. and F.W. Gingrich, **A Greek-English Lexicon of the New Testament.**
Barclay, William, **Flesh and Spirit.**
The Bible, American Standard Version.
The Bible, King James Version.
The Bible, New American Standard Bible.
The Bible, New International Version.
The Bible, New King James Version
Hamilton, Clinton, **Truth Commentaries 1 Peter.**
Statistical Abstract of the United States 1998.
Thayer, J.H., **A Greek-English Lexicon of the New Testament.**
Theological Dictionary of the New Testament.
Trench, R.C., **Synonyms of the New Testament.**
Vine, W.E., **An Expository Dictionary of New Testament Words.**

Lesson Eleven:

The Reward of Ruth

Lesson

The period of the judges was a time of spiritual darkness, moral decay, economic hardship and political chaos in Israel. But this dark era had its bright spots, and no light of righteousness shone more beautifully in this midnight of sin than that which radiated from the life a poverty stricken young widow, Ruth the Moabitess.

She was not descended from Abraham but from the loathed descendants of Lot's son Moab, whom Lot fathered by incest with his elder daughter. (Genesis 19:30–37) A Moabite male or one descended from a Moabite male was never to be allowed to enter the congregation of the Lord. (Deuteronomy 23:3–4) Yet Boaz, a good hearted Israelite, blessed Ruth thus, "The Lord repay your work, and a full reward be given you by the Lord God of Israel, under whose wings you have come for refuge." (Ruth 2:12) Perhaps no woman before Mary received such full reward as did Ruth. Why was Ruth the Moabitess so greatly rewarded by the Lord God of Israel?

The Faithfulness of Ruth
chapter one

Sometime during the era of the judges, when there was famine throughout Israel, Elimelech, a native of Bethlehem in Judah, took his wife Naomi and their two sons, Mahlon and Chilion, to the land of Moab, and they became strangers in a foreign land seeking relief from the famine. Elimelech died there. Mahlon, the elder son, married a young Moabite woman named Ruth, and Chilion married the Moabitess Orpah. The law forbid Israelites to marry the Canaanite inhabitants of the Land of Promise (Deuteronomy 7:1–4), but it did not forbid marriage to Moabites. Tragically, within ten years of their arrival in Moab, both Mahlon and Chilion died also.

Poor Naomi. She who had been the wife of a land-owner in Judah, she who had two sons to love and who could support her in her old age, was now bereft of property, husband, and sons and was a refugee in a Gentile country.

When the decade of her sojourn in Moab had transpired, Naomi received word that the Lord had visited His people Israel by lifting the famine and giving them food. Thus, she determined to return to her home, Bethlehem. Ruth and Orpah were admirably faithful to Naomi and began with her the trek to Judah.

Naomi realized only too well that the worldly interests of her daughters-in-law lay, not with her, but with their mothers in Moab. Thus, Naomi gently advised Ruth and Orpah to return to their mothers' houses. She recognized they had been good wives, and invoked the Lord's blessings on them accordingly. She wished them to find rest from anxiety and want by marrying again, which constituted the only prospect for a secure existence in ancient times for a childless widow. She tenderly, affectionately kissed them goodby.

But both the young women wept aloud and stated their determination to go with Naomi to live with her people. What a wonderful mother-in-law Naomi must have been for these two young women to determine to follow her rather than to return to their own mothers.

But Naomi insistently stated that she had nothing of this world to offer the young women. The law of Moses demanded that, if a man died without an heir, his brother was to marry his widow. The first son born of this relationship was to be reckoned as the heir of the dead brother and was to inherit his land, so that land in Israel would remain within the family estate. (Deuteronomy 25:5–6) But, Naomi reasoned in rhetorical questions that, due to her age, she could not have more sons, and that, even if she could, the young women would not refrain from marriage until the boys grew to marriageable age. Naomi was grieved that her misfortune had become their misfortune.

Naomi was a good woman. She still believed in the one true God of Israel. But, as Job, her misfortune had caused doubt and bitterness to arise in her heart. She attributed her troubles to the Lord. She even counseled Ruth to return to the gods of Moab—Baal of Peor, worshipped by ritual harlotry (Numbers 25:1–3), and "Chemosh the abomination of Moab." (1 Kings 11:7) Sadly, Naomi had become bitter. When Naomi ("Pleasant") returned to Bethlehem, she told the people to call her "Mara." ("Bitter") When our faith is not strong enough to face adversity with confidence that the Lord will always do right, it causes us to become bitter, and to stumble and to become stumbling blocks to others.

Both the daughters-in-law wept aloud again. Orpah kissed Naomi goodby and returned home. But Ruth could not be dissuaded from following Naomi. She "clung" to her. This is the same word in Hebrew translated "joined" in Genesis 2:24 and used to describe the marriage tie.

Ruth the Moabitess, in her faithfulness, became a pillar of strength for her mother-in-law, though it was Naomi and her family who introduced Ruth to the Lord. How often do spouses who grow up in worldly homes but are led to Christ by their mates become spiritually stronger than the family members who grew up worshipping the Lord.

Naomi entreated Ruth to follow her sister-in-law and return to Moab. But, in immortal, beautiful words of faithfulness Ruth emphatically stated her determination.

> "Entreat me not to leave you,
> Or to turn back from following after you;
> For wherever you go, I will go;
> And wherever you lodge, I will lodge;
> Your people shall be my people,
> And your God, my God.
> Where you die, I will die,
> And there will I be buried.
> The Lord do so to me, and more also,
> If anything but death parts you and me." (1:16–17)

This beautiful oath has often been used by a brides as a wedding vow, and, even though it was spoken by a daughter-in-law to her mother-in-law, the sentiment is still appropriate to marriage. This is particularly true since Ruth clung to Naomi as a wife to her husband. She invoked death upon herself if anything but death parted her from Naomi. She would even die and be buried among the people of Naomi.

Was Ruth just faithful to Naomi, or was she faithful to the Lord God as well? She took her oath of the Lord (17b), as the law demanded. (Deuteronomy 6:13) Boaz later commended Ruth for placing her trust in "the Lord God of Israel." (2:12) Yes, Ruth was faithful to Naomi, but the lives of Mahlon and Naomi had led Ruth to faithfulness to God, even as our lives should lead our loved ones and friends to be faithful to Christ. (Matthew 5:16) Ruth's vow was appropriate because Naomi served the Lord, and her vow is appropriate of the bride in a wedding today only if the groom is a Christian and because he is a Christian.

Naomi, realizing Ruth's determination, ceased trying to dissuade her, and they traveled to Bethlehem together. Fortunately, they arrived at the beginning of the barley harvest, which was the first crop to be harvested, in early April.

Ruth is a great example of faithfulness, steadfast loyalty to both the Lord and one's family, through the most difficult of adversity.

The Service of Ruth
chapter two

The law made provisions for the unfortunate by demanding that, when Israelites harvested their crops, they were to leave the corners of the fields unharvested and not go back and pick up what they had dropped or overlooked, but leave this for the poor to glean. (Leviticus 19:9–10; 23:22; Deuteronomy 24:19–21) Thus, the poor could maintain themselves by honorable labor.

Ruth was not too lazy to do hard work in the field, nor was she too proud to engage in menial labor. She humbly asked permission from Naomi to go into the fields around Bethlehem to glean, and Naomi lovingly granted her request.

Ruth by chance happened to glean in the field of Boaz. Boaz was a wealthy, older man, kin to Elimelech, Naomi's husband. He was a man of faith who maintained a good relationship with his workers.

When Boaz inquired of his foreman about Ruth, he identified her as the young Moabitess who had come with Naomi from Moab. The foreman commended her politeness for asking permission to glean and her industrious work in the field.

Boaz showed his own goodness of heart by requesting Ruth to remain in his fields gleaning throughout the harvest. He commanded the young men who labored for him not to molest her in any way and gave her permission to drink of the water that had been drawn for his workers.

In sincere humility Ruth prostrated herself before gentle Boaz and wondered aloud that he should favor her and show such kindness to a foreigner. After all, she was different from his maidservants. Oh, that all were as kind to those of different races, nationalities, and ethnic groups as Boaz was to Ruth.

Boaz explained that he had heard all about her and how she had forsaken her own land and people to remain loyal to Naomi and to the Lord. In magnificent expression of faith, Boaz, the respected, gentleman farmer invoked upon poor, young Ruth the full reward of the Lord for her obedient trust in Him. "God is not unjust to forget your work and labor of love." (Hebrews 6:10)

Humble Ruth simply requested that she continue to find favor from Boaz. She spoke wonderingly of his kindness and gratefully of the comfort she had received. The rest, that Naomi in her bitterness had directed Ruth to find from her Moabite kin and gods, Ruth had found in Israel by placing her trust in the Lord.

Ruth's character had won for her the admiration and kind attention of good-hearted Boaz. He shared his lunch with her, giving her more than she could eat. He even directed the laborers to allow her to glean without rebuke among the sheaves and to allow some of the grain to fall purposely from the bundles that she could glean them. Thus, her harvest was increased without her self respect being injured. Kind Boaz was even carefully considerate of the feelings of the godly, young Moabitess.

Ruth worked all day in the field of Boaz and gleaned an ephah (20–25 pounds) of barley, enough to last Naomi and her several days. She dutifully gave Naomi all except what she had eaten already.

Naomi realized that someone had paid special attention to Ruth, else she could not have fared so well in her gleaning. She excitedly inquired where Ruth had labored, and Ruth replied, "The man's name with whom I worked today is Boaz."

Naomi suddenly realized with joy that the Lord had not forsaken her or the family of her husband and son. Her complaint that God had dealt bitterly with her was transformed into praise to Him who had "not forsaken His kindness." Naomi knew what Ruth could not have realized. Boaz was a near kinsman! Naomi, in the desperate straits to which she had been reduced, had been forced to sell the field that belonged to her husband Elimelech and that had passed on to Mahlon and Chilion upon Elimelech's death. (4:3,9) But the law of Moses did not allow any family to permanently lose their hereditary estate. Every fifty years was a "Jubilee," in which each family could return to their inherited possession. (Leviticus 25:10) The land could not be permanently sold but was priced according to the number of crop years before the next Jubilee. (Leviticus 25:13–16) To further insure that families did not fall into permanent poverty in Israel, the law allowed the nearest kinsman of one who had to sell his land due to poverty to redeem (buy back) the land for his poor kinsman. (Leviticus 25:23–25) What thoughts of joy and wonder must have raced through Naomi's head and found blessed expression on her tongue as she suddenly realized the Lord had not abandoned her or her family after all!

Ruth informed Naomi that Boaz had requested her to glean in his fields throughout the harvest, and Naomi encouraged her to follow that very plan. Ruth did so throughout both the barley and wheat harvests, which lasted into June.

Ruth's faithfulness found expression in humble service. She worked hard without vain pride at sweaty, menial labor to provide for herself and her mother-in-law. This did not go unnoticed or unappreciated by godly people or, above all, by the Lord. The reward of her steadfastness led her mother-in-law to overcome her bitterness and to turn to God in praise for His kindness.

The Obedience of Ruth
chapter 3

Apparently Israelite custom had extended the obligation to marry a childless widow beyond the brothers to near kinsmen and had combined this with the near kinsman's right to redeem the land of an impoverished relative. (Ruth 3:9; 4:5) Based on these customs, Naomi, in gratitude to her faithful daughter-in-law and renewed confidence in the Lord, conceived a bold plan to provide security for Ruth.

The time had come for the harvested grain to be winnowed. On the site where the grain had been extracted from the husk by threshing, the intermingled refuse and grain would be tossed into the air by the winnowing fan, that the heavier grain might fall back to the threshing floor as the lighter husks and stalks were scattered by the wind. At the end of the day, the paid laborers and gleaners would retire to their homes, and the owners of the fields would sleep with their precious harvest to guard it. Thus, Boaz would be sleeping alone on his threshing floor.

Naomi advised Ruth to prepare herself to be attractive, go to the threshing floor of Boaz, wait until he was asleep, and to fold the cover back from his feet, lie down at his feet, and wait for him to tell her what to do. Naomi could only advise this because of complete confidence in the purity of both Ruth and Boaz. But the move would expose Ruth to the possibility of an embarrassing rejection, the loss of Boaz's good will on which they both depended, and even the loss of her good reputation. It would take great courage for Ruth to obey her mother-in-law.

But Ruth did not hesitate. She responded, "All that you say to me I will do." Ruth obediently "did according to all that her mother-in-law instructed her."

Boaz ate a good meal, lay down cheerfully next to his harvest, and fell fast asleep. Ruth quietly came, uncovered his feet and laid down. Boaz awoke at midnight and was startled to discover someone lying at his feet. He urgently inquired, "Who are you?" Ruth gently replied, "I am Ruth, your maidservant. Take your maidservant under your wing, for you are a close relative." Boaz was the human agent by whom the Lord provided for Ruth. (cf. 2:12)

Rather than taking offense, Boaz was filled with gratitude, and his gratitude was expressed in a beautiful blessing. The older man addressed her as his daughter. He recognized that she had been kind to him in seeking marriage to him rather than a young man and kind to her deceased husband in seeking to perpetuate his name and his estate. He promised to fulfill her request.

The final reason Boaz gave for being willing to marry Ruth was one of the greatest sincere compliments ever paid to a woman. He explained, "for all the people of my town know that you are a virtuous woman." Perhaps some would object to the description of a virtuous woman in Proverbs 31:10–31 by contending, This is the unrealistic description of an ideal woman; no real woman was ever like that.

Perhaps others would object, Proverbs 31 are the thoughts of a queen and the description of a wealthy, Israelite woman, and the passage does not apply to common people. But there was one—only one—actual woman described in the Scriptures by the Hebrew word "virtuous," the very same word found in Proverbs 31:10. She was a poor, Gentile widow named Ruth, who came for refuge under the wings of the Lord God of Israel. She was real, she was neither royal nor wealthy, and she was not a Jew. She was the living example of and is the real pattern for the virtuous woman.

But Boaz was not only gentle and kind, he was also righteous. He knew there was a kinsman who was closer relation to Elimelech than he and who thus had the first right to redeem Elimelech's property and to marry Ruth. Boaz directed Ruth to stay where she was through the night. He swore by the Lord that he would perform the duty of the redeemer if the nearer relative did not.

Ruth rose before it was light enough to see. To protect both their reputations, Boaz instructed her to remain silent about the night's business. He placed six measures of barley into her shawl for her to carry home, and Ruth returned to Naomi in Bethlehem.

Naomi wisely advised Ruth to remain quietly at home, for she knew that Boaz would find no rest until the matter had been settled.

Ruth was obedient to everything she was commanded, even though her obedience led her into the possibility of rejection, embarrassment, and disgrace. She is the living example of a virtuous women.

The Reward of Ruth
chapter four

Boaz, in the meanwhile, went to the gate of Bethlehem, inside which all the public affairs of the city were transacted. Eventually the nearer kinsman happened by, and Boaz politely requested him to sit down. Then Boaz assembled twelve elders of the city as witnesses and proceeded to state his business.

Just Boaz informed the nearer kinsman that Naomi had sold the land belonging to Elimelech, Mahlon and Chilion, and that, as the only kinsman nearer to Elimelech than Boaz, he had the right of redemption. As the matter stood, the nearer kinsman had the opportunity to increase his own estate and wealth, and he readily agreed to redeem the land.

But then Boaz informed him of a condition. When he redeemed the land, the widow of Mahlon, Ruth, went with the land to be his in marriage. This would mean that the first son born to their union would be the heir of Mahlon and would receive as his inheritance the field the kinsman had bought. Thus, the redeemer would detract from the value of his own land by using its produce to buy the field and would have nothing from the field for his own permanent estate. The kinsman immediately changed his mind and asked Boaz to redeem the land. The nearer kinsman did not violate the law. He did not have to redeem the land or marry Ruth. He just acted from self interest, lacking the kindness and generosity of Boaz.

To seal the transaction, the nearer kinsman observed the ancient custom in Israel of taking off his shoe and handing it to Boaz before the witnesses. Thus, he had transferred to Boaz the right to walk on the land as his own. Boaz announced before the witnesses that the transaction was complete. He had acquired the land Naomi had sold, and he had acquired Ruth as his wife, that he might raise up an heir to Elimelech and Mahlon, that their names might not cease in Israel.

The witnesses and townspeople who had gathered round all instantly recognized both the righteousness and the kindness of Boaz's actions. They not only confirmed the business but pronounced upon Boaz a great blessing. Boaz was a descendant of Judah from the family of Perez, Judah's son by the Canaanite woman Tamar. (Genesis 38) The people blessed Boaz by wishing that Ruth would increase his house as Rachel and Leah had increased Jacob's and as Tamar had increased Judah's.

Boaz and Ruth were married, and the Lord blessed them with a son. But the one who received the most congratulations was Naomi. The women blessed the Lord for giving Naomi a true near kinsman, this little grandson, and they wished for him fame and for Naomi that the child would restore life to her family and care for her in her old age. They praised Ruth for her love for her mother-in-law. Indeed, they exclaimed, in true Hebrew hyperbole, that this Moabite daughter-in-law was better to Naomi than seven sons!

Naomi had the joy of nursing her grandson. The women called him Naomi's son and named him "Obed," "the serving one," for he would dutifully serve the needs of his aged grandmother.

The greatest fulfillment of womanhood is in bearing and raising children, and the greatest joy of mothers is the accomplishments of their children. How Ruth was blessed! Her great grandson was David, the greatest king of Israel, and from her was descended the Christ, the Savior of the world.

This poor Moabite widow was the living example of a virtuous woman. She was faithful to her husband, mother-in-law and the Lord. She humbly served in hard, menial labor. She was obedient under trying circumstances. She took refuge under the wings of the Lord, and He gave her rest, security from want and anxiety. He blessed her with a loving, kind husband, a good name, and a son. Of women, only Mary received greater honor, as Ruth became the ancestor of both David and Christ. Truly, she was given a full reward by the Lord God of Israel.

Questions

I. List of Passages Used in This Lesson (Read each passage and be able to discuss its meaning and its application to the lesson.)

> The Book of Ruth
> Genesis 19:30–37
> Deuteronomy 23:3–4
> Deuteronomy 7:1–4
> Numbers 25:1–3
> 1 Kings 11:7
> Genesis 2:24
> Deuteronomy 6:13

> Matthew 5:16
> Leviticus 19:9–10
> Leviticus 23:22
> Deuteronomy 24:19–21
> Hebrews 6:10
> Leviticus 25:10,13–16,23–25
> Genesis 38

II. Terms to Define

1. Naomi

2. Mara

3. clung

4. ephah

5. Jubilee

6. redeem

7. Obed

III. Fact Questions

1. How did Israelites regard Moabites?

2. Tell in your own words the story of Naomi and Ruth up to the time they returned to Bethlehem.

3. How did the law provide that a man who died without an heir might receive an heir?

4. Relate how Ruth went to glean and the results.

5. How did the law of Moses make provisions for feeding the poor?

6. How did the law guarantee that no Israelite family was permanently without land?

7. Describe the bold plan of Naomi that Ruth followed to become Boaz's wife?

8. Tell how Boaz obtained Ruth as his wife.

IV. Thought Questions

1. Did Naomi do right when she advised Ruth and Orpah to return to Moab?

2. What kind of relationship did Naomi have with her daughters-in-law?

3. How can mothers-in-law and daughters-in-law have this kind of relationship?

4. What kind of outlook on life had Naomi acquired by the time she returned to Bethlehem?

5. Was her attitude justified?

6. Is it proper to use Ruth 1:16-17 as a bridal wedding vow?

7. Was Ruth just faithful to Naomi, or was she also faithful to the Lord?

8. How does Ruth exemplify humble service?

9. What kind of man was Boaz?

10. Why did the news of Ruth's work in the field of Boaz cause Naomi to change her attitude?

11. How did Ruth demonstrate obedience?

12. What blessings did Ruth bring to Naomi?

V. Discussion

1. How is Ruth an example of:

    a. faithfulness?

    b. service?

    c. obedience?

2. In what ways is she the remarkable pattern of a virtuous woman?

3. How did the Lord reward Ruth?

Lesson Twelve:

Esther

Lesson

We now leap forward several hundred years in time from Ruth and are transported over seven hundred miles across Syria and Mesopotamia to the Persian royal city of Shushan (Susa), the site of the splendid winter palace of the king, to consider the delightful story of Esther. In the early fifth century before Christ, Persia was the most powerful and extensive kingdom on earth, stretching from Libya and Macedonia in the West to India in the East and occupying portions of three continents, the greatest Middle Eastern empire which had ever existed to that time. Xerxes (Ahasuerus) was the mighty king of kings who came to the throne of Persia on the death of his father Darius in 486. He was proud, despotic, capricious, fickle, reckless of human lives, and given to sensual pleasure, had crushed revolt in Egypt and lived in unmatched splendor in Shushan. His rule was absolute, and his laws unchangeable.

The Jews had been allowed to return to their homeland from captivity by Xerxes' grandfather Cyrus, but many thousands of God's people still remained scattered throughout the empire. Among them was Mordecai, who served in the court of the king in Susa. He was raising his orphaned cousin Hadassah (Esther), who was a young woman with a remarkably beautiful face and figure.

The lives of the great king and the orphan girl soon became intertwined to form the fabric of the story of the greatest danger God's Old Testament people ever faced and their deliverance by an orphan who became queen. Esther is a superlative example of one who courageously accepted the challenge set before her by the providence of God. She is a true national heroine on the scale of Joan of Arc and a great example to both women and men.

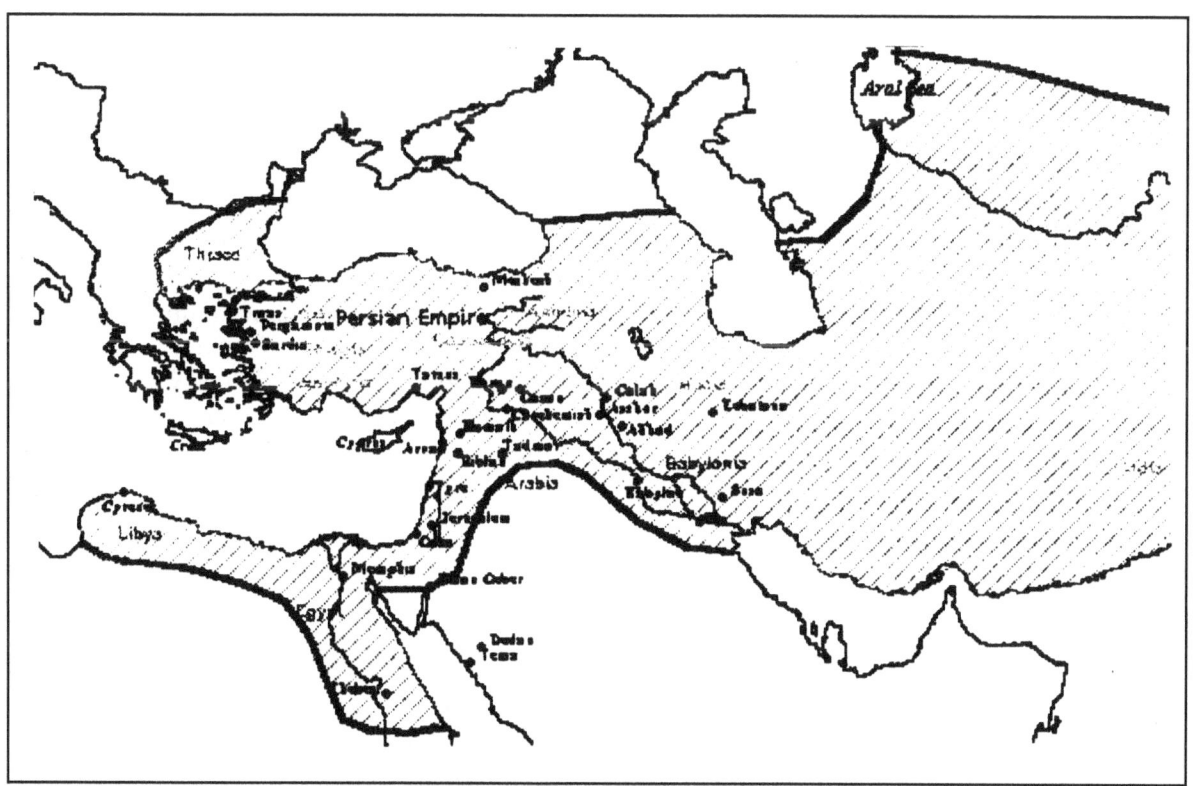

What a remarkable book Esther is! It is the only book of the Bible which never mentions God, yet His providential care for His people, not just in Palestine but throughout the world, is its theme. The book of Esther does not record a single miracle, yet the hand of God is behind every event. The story never refers to prayer, but doubtless millions of prayers were answered. The Word of God is never mentioned, yet Mordecai was a strict observer of that Word. What a perfect picture of the unseen but ever present providential hand of God.

The Feast of Ahasuerus (chapter 1)

In the year 483 Xerxes was making preparation for the conquest of the pesky Greek city states which had turned back his father Darius. The satraps (rulers) and lower officials from all 120 Persian provinces were gathered in Susa for six months so they could help the king plan the invasion and be feasted by him and so the king could vainly display his awesome wealth. As the last grand spectacle Ahasuerus feasted all the inhabitants of Susa for a week. The men assembled in the monumental 60,000 square foot garden court, sheltered from the sun by blue and white awnings, hung by linen cords from silver rods. The court pillars were of marble, and the pavement was of various colored stone. They reclined to eat and drink on gold and silver couches, and drank from golden cups, each of a distinct design. The king supplied all the wine anyone cared to drink, but no one was required to drink any more than he desired.

At the same time, in accordance with Persian custom for men and women to dine separately on public occasions, Queen Vashti (probably the queen known to the Greeks as Amestris) feasted the women apart in the palace.

On the last day of the feast, the king, under the influence of wine, summoned the queen to appear before the audience of revelrous, sated men to display her great beauty. In Persia, for any woman to so appear was immodest, and the demand was an affront to the dignity of a queen. The very man who should have protected Vashti's modesty and dignity, because of the influence of wine, demanded that she sacrifice both to his vain conceit. Vashti was neither the first nor last wife to suffer indignity from a drinking husband or because of a husband's foolish pride.

Vashti showed courage, and perhaps stubborn haughtiness as well, and refused to so display herself. Such contempt for the word of the king was unthinkable in Persia, even by the queen. King Xerxes was furious, and his anger would not subside. In the crowning hour of his greatest display of arrogant vanity, he was belittled before his adoring subjects by his own wife. His enormous pride was deeply hurt.

At least the king had the good sense to seek advice before he acted to retaliate. He sought the counsel of the heads of the seven Persian families who were his closest advisors.

Memucan spoke of the effect that the queen's behavior would have on Persian households. (No one mentioned how the king's behavior set a bad example.) Wives would be encouraged to defy their husbands. The contempt the wives would show to their husbands would cause the husbands to react in anger. Domestic trouble would result. In one sense these men were wiser than many national leaders today, since they recognized that when wives treat their husbands with contempt, many husbands react violently. Wife abuse is inexcusable and intolerable, but its increase directly parallels the rise of the women's liberation movement.

Thus, the decree went forth throughout Persia. Vashti was deposed as queen. Men were recognized as the rulers of their own homes. The husband's native tongue was to be spoken at home if his wife were of another nationality.

The Feasts of Esther (chapters two through seven)

Some time after this, when his anger had subsided, the vain king began to pine for Vashti. So his fawning attendants suggested he have a "Miss Persia" contest with the king as the sole judge and crown the winner Queen of Persia. Each maiden was to have a year in the section of the harem where the virgins were kept to be beautified and purified to spend one night with King Ahasuerus. He was delighted with the idea, and beautiful, young virgins from around Persia were assembled.

Esther was one of the chosen virgins and, along with the others, was committed to the care of Hegai, the eunuch in charge of the virgins. Hegai was immediately impressed with Esther and gave her seven of the best attendants to wait on her, moved her to the best place in the women's quarters and gave her additional beauty preparations.

All of this could have gone to Esther's head, but, even in the harem, Esther continued to heed the commands her loving guardian Mordecai had given her. In obedience to him, she did not reveal that she was a Jew. Mordecai daily walked by the women's quarters, seeking news of his beloved Esther.

When it came Esther's turn to go into the king's chamber, she took only those things with her that Hegai provided. Everyone who saw her was impressed with her beauty. This included King Xerxes, who loved her more than any of the other virgins. He chose Esther to be queen, set the royal crown upon her head, and made a great feast in her honor for all his officials, which people remembered as Esther's Feast. He even proclaimed a holiday throughout the empire and gave generous gifts. Esther became queen in the seventh year of Ahasuerus' reign, 479 BC, which was soon after he returned from Greece, bitterly disappointed with disgraceful defeat and seeking solace in the pleasures of his harem.

Later more young virgins were brought to Shushan to be included in the king's harem. Mordecai was sitting "within the king's gate" at the time. No one in the palace knew the kinship of Mordecai and Esther, for, even though Esther was now queen, she still obeyed Mordecai's commands as she did when a child. "The royal dignity did not change Esther's heart. She was still the dutiful child she had been so many years." (Rawlinson. 55)

In a case of palace intrigue, similar to that which eventually led to the death of Xerxes, Mordecai learned that two eunuchs in the especially trusted position of keeping the door of the king's bed chamber had become angry with Ahasuerus and were plotting his murder. He informed Esther, who in turn informed the king, naming Mordecai as her informant but not revealing their relationship. An investigation confirmed the charge, and the two attendants involved in the murderous plot were executed. Since Mordecai had rendered an especially important service that would demand a proper reward, the king personally attended the recording of the event by the chroniclers.

Several years later wicked, vain Haman was elevated to the post of grand vizier, a position second only to the king in affairs of state. The king commanded his subjects to bow and pay homage to Haman, but Mordecai refused to give the worshipful homage to a man that should be given to God alone. The king's servants remonstrated with Mordecai daily to obey the command and wanted to know why he disobeyed. He simply told them he was a Jew.

They desired to know if this reason would stand up, so they informed Haman that Mordecai refused to pay him homage. When Haman learned of Mordecai's refusal to venerate him, he was very angry, and when he was informed of the reason, he decided to extract vengeance, not just on Mordecai, but on the entire Jewish people. His arrogance was such that he would without hesitation destroy a whole race of people for the slight of one man.

At the beginning of the Jewish year, in the twelfth year of Xerxes' reign, BC 474, Haman cast lots (like rolling dice) to determine the lucky time for the execution of his plot. As was Persian custom, and the custom of unbelievers today, Haman thought events were in the hands of fate and sought to have good luck. He settled on the thirteenth day of the twelfth month as the lucky day to carry out the genocide. Thus, the Jews had almost a year to prepare and to fear.

Haman went to the king and defamed the Jews as a people scattered throughout his empire whose laws were diverse from all other people and whose very existence was against the king's interests. Of course, the first part of his charge was true. Haman offered Xerxes 10,000 talents, equal to about two-thirds of the king's annual revenue, to let him bring about the destruction of all the Jews. He promised Xerxes that all the money and property confiscated from this people would go into the king's treasury.

This was indeed a tempting proposition for a despotic king who had no feeling for subjected peoples and whose treasury had been recently depleted by the disastrous war with the Greeks. So he turned his signet ring over to Haman, which gave the wicked vizier the authority to issue a decree in the king's name, giving Haman the authority to do as he saw fit with the Jews.

Haman chose the "lucky" thirteenth day of the month, the first month, to issue the decree that all the Jews, young and old, male and female, were to be annihilated. All the rulers throughout the empire were obligated to help carry out the heinous orders. The decree was written in the languages of all peoples of the empire and carried by the king's messengers to every corner of Persian territories. The entire Jewish race was to be exterminated in one day. Their fate seemed sealed.

The city of Shushan was disturbed and thrown into confusion, but wicked Haman and despotic Xerxes, with no feeling for the fate of millions of subjects, simply sat down to eat.

When Mordecai learned of the decree he put on sackcloth and heaped ashes on his head as signs of deep grief and went into the city wailing loudly. He could only go as far as the gate of the palace in this condition, for no private sorrow was to bother the king. Throughout Persia the Jews lamented.

Within the secluded world of the harem, Esther knew nothing of these affairs. However, word came to Esther through the eunuchs and her attendants of Mordecai's public mourning. In her concern for her beloved Mordecai, she tore her clothes in anguish and sent him proper clothing, perhaps that he might be able to come into the palace and tell her the reason for his grief.

Mordecai refused the clothing but sent word to Esther informing her of the terrible events that were happening. He directed her to go to the king and make supplication for the Jews.

But Esther returned word to Mordecai that she herself faced a private dilemma. The king's rule was so absolute that no one, not even the queen, could enter his presence unbidden. If anyone did so, unless he held out the royal golden scepter to welcome them, they would be put to death. The king had not sent for Esther in thirty days. She was afraid she had fallen out of favor. If she ventured into the throne room unbidden, she could forfeit her life.

The following passage (Esther 4:13–16) is the heart of the book and contains great lessons and examples of immense value to all people in every age. Mordecai returned word to Esther that, if she did not speak to the king, deliverance would arise for the Jews from another quarter, but she would perish along with her father's family. "Yet who knows," he mused, "whether you have come to the kingdom for such a time as this?" With courage that exceeded even her beauty, the queen, still obedient to her guardian, determined to do her duty even if it meant death. But now, as queen, she commanded her subjects, Mordecai and the Jews of Shushan, to fast for her three days, and she and her female attendants would likewise fast, after which she would take the fateful step to go before the king. Mordecai obeyed his queen.

We pause in our story here to observe three great lessons. While Mordecai had unshakable faith in God's care for his people, he did not venture to assign any specific event to that divine providence. When Esther learned that her position placed upon her unique responsibility, she courageously accepted that duty and determined to fulfill it. Then she sought the help of God through fasting to accomplish His will.

When the fateful day arrived, Esther donned her royal apparel and crossed over to the king's palace, where his throne faced the entrance to the

Three Lessons

- 📖 **Believe in providence, but do not assign specific events in your life to providence.**
- 📖 **When you learn your duty, have the courage to do it.**
- 📖 **Seek God's help to do His will.**

★ **Men of small character often attain great power and influence.**

★ **High honors and position do not guarantee happiness or peace of mind.**

hall. When Xerxes saw Esther he welcomed her by extending the scepter, and she touched its top in submission to his rule. Recognizing that Esther must have a request of great importance to take such a risk, the king asked her petition and promised to give her up to half the kingdom. She asked only one very unusual favor, that the king and Haman come that day to the feast she had prepared. This was further indication she had important business with her husband, for Persian kings and their queens usually dined separately, and neither usually dined with their subjects.

King Ahasuerus and his grand vizier Haman attended Esther's banquet of wine. Again the king asked what her request was. Perhaps through hesitance to speak to the king of so important a subject, Esther asked that the king and Haman attend another feast the next day, and she promised to then make known her petition.

What an honor had been bestowed on Haman! He alone dined with both the king and queen and was invited to do so again the next day. How his vain heart was lifted up with pride. He left the presence of the royal couple in joy, but when he passed Mordecai in the entrance to the palace, Mordecai didn't even show the respect of standing up for him, and he certainly didn't tremble in affected fear as the other attendants. Arrogant Haman was furious.

He returned home to his wife Zeresh and their friends. He boasted to them of all his honors and accomplishments, yet he lamented that they meant nothing to him as long as he had to endure the impertinence of Mordecai. Men of small character often attain positions of great power and influence. High honors and position cannot guarantee happiness or peace of mind.

Zeresh and their friends had the solution to Haman's problem. Build a gallows 75 feet high, request the king to have Mordecai hanged on it, and then go merrily to the banquet with the king. Ah, such sweet revenge. Make a grand spectacle of the humiliating death of one who dared not fawn at your feet. Such coldness of heart. Kill your enemy and go off merrily to feast. The plan suited Haman well, and he had Haman's gallows erected.

But seemingly unconnected events began to come together to defeat Haman. That very night the king could not sleep. He commanded the chronicles of his reign to be read. (That should have put anyone to sleep.) The reader happened to come to the favor that Mordecai had bestowed upon the king by saving him from the plot of his two eunuchs. It was very important under Persian law and custom that the king generously reward such a favor. The king earnestly inquired what reward had been given to Mordecai, and the answer was, "None."

But morning had arrived. Haman, eager to seek Mordecai's death, stood outside in the court, waiting to ask the king to hang Mordecai.

Xerxes sent for Haman and asked, "What shall be done for the man whom the king delights to honor?" In his unbounded vanity, Haman could think of no one the king would want to honor more than himself. In his arrogance, he could think of nothing greater than public honors.

And Haman answered the king, "For the man whom the king delights to honor, let a royal robe be brought which the king has worn, and a horse on which the king has ridden, which has a royal crest placed on its head. Then let this robe and horse be delivered to the hand of one of the king's most noble princes, that he may array the man whom the king delights to honor. Then parade him on horseback through the city square, and proclaim before him: 'Thus shall it be done to the man whom the king delights to honor!'"

Each of these acts were such honors that, had not the king granted permission, they would have brought the death penalty.

> *Then the king said to Haman, "Hurry, take the robe and the horse, as you have suggested, and do so for Mordecai the Jew who sits within the king's gate! Leave nothing undone of all that you have spoken."*

Such mortification! The honors Haman thought to have bestowed upon himself, he himself was to bestow on his hated enemy. The enemy whom he thought to have the king hang, the king had Haman give the highest honors.

Haman obeyed the king and then in complete humiliation rushed home with his face covered. With utter anguish he told his wife and advisors what had transpired. In their superstitious trust in fate and luck, they warned that, if indeed Mordecai was a Jew, since Haman had begun to fall before him, he would surely be defeated by Mordecai.

Before they could even finish their discussion, the king's messengers arrived to escort Haman to the banquet with the king and queen.

King Ahasuerus and the now anxious Haman came to dine with Esther. Once again Ahasuerus asked the queen to state her request and eagerly promised her anything she desired, up to half the kingdom. When the courage borne by determination and dedication to duty opened Esther's mouth and loosed her tongue to express her entreaty, words burst forth with the eloquence of emotion that stunned the king and filled the evil heart of Haman with panic.

> *Then Queen Esther answered and said, "If I have found favor in your sight, O king, and if it pleases the king, let my life be given me at my petition, and my people at my request. "For we have been sold, my people and I, to be destroyed, to be killed, and to be annihilated. Had we been sold as male and female slaves, I would have held my tongue, although the enemy could never compensate for the king's loss."*

Esther's request sought not just her own good but that of the king as well. Selling the Jews as slaves might have enriched the king's treasury, and Esther would have remained silent. But no amount of money could replace the loss of hundreds of thousands of loyal subjects whose industry supplied taxes to the king's coffers annually.

Neither the king nor Haman had imagined that Esther was a Jewess. Haman could not have known that his evil plot to extract vengeance for the slights of one man by the destruction of an entire race involved the death of the queen.

Incredulously the king demanded to know who would dare to presume to commit such a vile deed. Queen Esther replied in an instant, "The adversary and enemy is this wicked Haman!"

Haman was terrified. The king in fury arose and strode into the palace garden, perhaps to compose himself. Haman desperately rose to use this opening to plead for his life, and in panic fell upon the queen's couch to entreat mercy. Just then the king returned and, seeing Haman thus, inquired in shocked disbelief, "Will he also assault the queen while I am in the house?"

The servants immediately covered Haman's head, the sign he was a condemned man to be executed. Harbonah, one of the king's eunuch's, informed the king there was a gallows in Haman's house 75 feet high that Haman had planned to hang Mordecai on. (It doesn't appear Haman was popular with the court.) The king indignantly replied, "Hang him on it!" Haman was hanged on the gallows that he himself had built, and the king's anger was satisfied.

What grim justice! Haman's evil plan had turned upon him to his own destruction. The proverbial expression "hanged on Haman's gallows" has been used in the ages since to describe a wicked plan that backfires on its perpetrator. In reality, all wicked plots eventually backfire on the designer, either here or in eternity.

All wicked plots eventually backfire on the designer, either here or in eternity.

The Feast of Purim (chapters 8–10)

In Persian law, when a criminal was executed, all his property was confiscated by the government. Thus, on the death of Haman, all his property and household passed to the king, and the king recovered his signet ring. Ahasuerus immediately conferred Haman's property upon Queen Esther. Esther revealed to her husband Mordecai's kinship, and Mordecai became a high official with full access to the king. In fact, the king bestowed upon him the signet ring Haman had borne, giving him the power to enact laws in the king's name which Haman had possessed. And Esther gave Mordecai charge over Haman's house.

But the decree for the slaughter of the Jews was still in place. Thus, Queen Esther once more ventured before the king in the throne room, falling down at his feet and imploring with tears for the lives of her countrymen. Once again the king held out the golden scepter in approval of her presence. King Ahasuerus could not nullify his edict, since the laws of the Persian kings were irrevocable. But he gave Esther and Mordecai permission to authorize the Jews to defend themselves against their attackers on the fateful day and even to kill those who assaulted them and to confiscate their property. So Mordecai issued the command in the name of the king, sealed it with the royal signet ring and sent it with haste by messengers on swift horses to all the rulers of the Empire.

The results of the reversal of fortune were wonderful to behold. Mordecai did the king's business wearing the blue and white robe of nobility and a gold crown. The Jews were overjoyed and proclaimed a holiday, and they were honored by the peoples of Persia. In fact, many people were proselytized to Judaism as the result, and people were in fear of the Jews.

When the fateful day arrived, the day Haman's advisers had superstitiously chosen as the "lucky" day, the thirteenth day of the twelfth month (This was the month Adar, and the day is in early spring about a month before the Passover), Haman's scheme turned on his own family and all the enemies of the Jews. With permission from King Ahasuerus and with the help and cooperation of the Persian rulers, the Jews defended themselves against all who attacked them. In Shushan they killed 500 of their enemies and all ten of Haman's sons. Throughout the empire 75,000 enemies of the Jews were slain. This was indeed a large one day war. But, although the king had granted them the property and wealth of their enemies, the Jews did not take any spoils of war. With permission from the king, the Jews in Shushan defended themselves on the fourteenth day of the month as well, killing another 300 enemies, and the bodies of Haman's sons were hung publicly as a warning to all who would oppose the Jews. In celebration of this great victory, Queen Esther and Mordecai decreed that the fourteenth and fifteenth days of Adar would be a holiday, with feasting, gladness and exchanging of presents. This great holiday, which the Jewish people still celebrate, was called "Purim" (lots), from the casting of lots in commemoration of the fact that Haman's plot to destroy the Jews backfired, causing the death of Haman, the shameful destruction of his family and the enemies of the Jews, and a great victory for the Jews. The twelfth day of the month is remembered today by the Jews with a fast in memory of the fast of Esther and her attendants, Mordecai, and the Jews of Susa.

King Xerxes continued to reign over the vast expanse of lands from the islands of the Aegean Sea in the West to India in the East, exacting tribute from them. Mordecai was second only to the king in authority in all this enormous empire. His administration was beneficent and popular, especially to the Jews, and brought them peace.

Lessons

The book of Esther implies rather than states important principles. It is perhaps the supreme study in Scripture of the providence of God. From it we learn by case history that God, not mindless fate, rules the world. He rules in the affairs of men, from determining the rise and fall of nations to watching over and caring for an orphan girl of a conquered people who were outcasts in a foreign land. He cares for His people wherever they are and however insignificant they might seem.

> **Lessons from Esther**
>
> ★ **God, not mindless fate, rules the world.**
> ★ **He cares for his people.**
> ★ **Though His hand is unseen, He is there.**
> ★ **He has a plan for the life of everyone.**
> ★ **We must use the abilities we have to do God's will in our own situations.**
> ★ **Do not fight schemes with schemes.**
> ★ **Do not try to manipulate your husband or scheme to get your way.**

Events that at first seemed disconnected and random and are completely explainable by natural means become knit together in a beautiful picture of the unseen hand of God acting providentially in human affairs. Vashti is deposed as queen. A Jewish orphan girl is chosen to replace her. Mordecai refuses to venerate Haman. Haman decides to destroy the Jews. Mordecai commands Esther not to reveal she is Jewish. Esther obeys. Mordecai learns of a plot to kill the king, and tells it to Esther, who reveals it to the king in Mordecai's name. The king fails to reward Mordecai. Mordecai happens to be standing in the way when Haman leaves the king, having secured the destruction of the Jews. Esther puts off a day the time to make her request of the king. The king can't sleep. He has the chronicles read. The chronicler reads of the service of Mordecai, which has not been rewarded. Haman comes in at that very time to seek Mordecai's death. Amazing coincidences? The unseen, providential hand of God.

He has a plan for the life of everyone, a plan that we accomplish by using the abilities He gives us to obey His revealed will, the Scriptures, in whatever circumstances we find ourselves. Doubtless the little orphan girl Esther never dared imagine that she would be the queen of the mightiest empire the world had ever seen and would deliver her beloved people from destruction. But her responsibility was to do her duty in the situation where she was found with the abilities God had given her. If we refuse to do our duty, God's plan will still be accomplished, but we will be destroyed. In carrying out His will, He does not violate the freedom of will of any person. You may not be beautiful, and you will probably never be a queen, but you have God-given abilities and opportunities, and you must fulfill your resultant responsibilities in your own situation. Who knows what wonderful results could one day follow?

Though her enemy was a scheming, powerful ruler who manipulated her husband the king with his machinations, Esther did not try to fight back with plots of her own. Her husband had absolute authority over her, even the right to have her executed, and she had real reason to doubt his affections. But she did not scheme to thwart his will or try to manipulate him, but, with the use of proper deference and tact, approached the problem in a straightforward, honest manner, in faith leaving the outcome in the hands of God.

Haman placed his trust in fate, luck and wicked intrigue. Esther trusted God, obedience to His will, and honest compliance with right. Haman is remembered as the evil schemer whose plots backfired to his own destruction. Esther is remembered as one of the great heroines of faith.

Questions

I. Reading Assignment

Read the book of Esther in one sitting to gain an overview of the story. Then read the lesson. Then read Esther one chapter at a time, the part of the lesson that deals with that chapter and answer the following questions as you finish each part of the reading.

II. Terms to Define

1. Pur

2. Purim

III. Place to Locate

Shushan

IV. Person to Identify

Ahasuerus

IV. Fact Questions

Each student should outline the story of Esther. Let one student tell the story in class in its entirety. When she is finished, have the other students add details she may have left out.

V. Thought Questions

1. Analyze the character of:

a. Ahasuerus

b. Vashti

c. Mordecai

d. Esther

e. Haman

2. What lessons do we learn from Esther about:

    a. the providence of God?

    b. God's plan for your life?

    c. how to deal with the schemes of wicked people?

    d. how to deal with your husband?

VI. Discussion

What practical lessons can we learn from Esther to help us:

1. improve our character,

2. learn to fulfill God's will for our lives, and

3. learn to have a deeper faith in God?

Work Cited

George Rawlinson, **The Pulpit Commentary**. 7. ("The Book of Esther")

Lesson Thirteen:

Mary

Lesson

Now in the sixth month the angel Gabriel was sent by God to a city of Galilee named Nazareth, to a virgin betrothed to a man whose name was Joseph, of the house of David. The virgin's name was Mary. And having come in, the angel said to her, "Rejoice, highly favored one, the Lord is with you; blessed are you among women! (Luke 1:26–28)

Now Mary arose in those days and went into the hill country with haste, to a city of Judah, and entered the house of Zacharias and greeted Elizabeth. And it happened, when Elizabeth heard the greeting of Mary, that the babe leaped in her womb; and Elizabeth was filled with the Holy Spirit. Then she spoke out with a loud voice and said, "Blessed are you among women, and blessed is the fruit of your womb! But why is this granted to me, that the mother of my Lord should come to me? For indeed, as soon as the voice of your greeting sounded in my ears, the babe leaped in my womb for joy." "Blessed is she who believed, for there will be a fulfillment of those things which were told her from the Lord." (Luke 1:39–45)

Certainly no woman prior to the establishment of the kingdom of God was so blessed as was Mary the mother of Jesus. She was a humble peasant from a despised village in rural, hilly Northern Palestine, but she became the mother of the Christ the Son of God. It was no accident that God chose her to be the mother of His only begotten Son. Her character was such that she was eminently fitted to care for and provide guidance for the Child born to her. We will study her life to find lessons and qualities of character applicable to us today.

Luke 1:26–38

When her cousin Elizabeth was six months pregnant with John, the angel Gabriel appeared to a poor virgin named Mary in the remote, obscure village of Nazareth, far off from Jerusalem, the center of Judaism, in the mountains of Galilee. She was engaged to a carpenter named Joseph. Engagement (espousal, betrothal) was far more serious to ancient Jews than it is to us. The promised maiden was already considered to be the wife of her fiancee, so that if she had sexual relations with another man, it was punishable by death. (Deuteronomy 22:23–24) It took a divorce to end this relationship. (Matthew 1:19)

It was startling enough to Mary to have an angel appear to her, but Gabriel's greeting was especially troubling, "Rejoice, highly favored one, the Lord is with you; blessed are you among women!" (verse 28) Mary deliberated in her mind the meaning of this greeting. Gabriel calmed Mary's fear with perhaps the most surprising announcement ever delivered to a woman. She had found favor with God and would conceive a child. That Child would be the Savior and King promised hundreds of years before by the great prophet Isaiah. He would indeed be great, in that He would at once be the Son of God, the Son of David, and He would rule on the throne of David. (cf. Isaiah 9:6–7)

We can well imagine how overwhelming this all was to the simple maiden, and she, with no apparent lack of faith urgently inquired how she, who had never had sexual relations with any man, could bear a son. The angel explained that the Holy Spirit would come upon her, and God's power would be manifested in her, and her Son would be the Son of God. As further reassurance, Gabriel told her that her aged, barren cousin Elizabeth was even at that time six months pregnant! The angel assured Mary, "For with God nothing will be impossible." (verse 37)

Two millennia before, God had promised aged Abraham and Sarah a son, and they had laughed in unbelief. (Genesis 17:15–19; 18:9–12) Only when the Lord had inquired rhetorically, "Is anything too hard for the Lord?" (Genesis 18:14), did Sarah learn to believe and laugh with joy at the birth of Isaac, whose very name means "laughter." (Genesis 21:1–7; cf. Hebrews 11:11)

But the maiden Mary with the credulity of simple, trusting faith and the humble submission of a dedicated servant of God simply replied to Gabriel, "Behold the maidservant of the Lord! Let it be to me according to your word." (verse 38) How trusting and self-sacrificing that reply was soon became obvious. Passive submission to God's will in difficult circumstances, which is often the lot of virtuous women, is just as much the obedience of faith as the active, public service which gains men renown.

In the earliest part of Mary's life that we have a record of her, she demonstrated moral purity, a more ready faith than even Abraham and Sarah, and humble submission to God's will. She had a quiet, contemplative disposition, which caused her to reflect upon the will of God and the significance of words, actions, and events. No wonder God highly favored her.

Luke 1:39–56

The most natural reaction on Mary's part would be to visit her cousin Elizabeth, whose condition Gabriel employed to bolster Mary's faith, both to share with her their mutual, uniquely feminine joy, and to have her faith reinforced by actually seeing Elizabeth in her condition. Thus, Mary quickly went to visit Elizabeth. It was no more wrong or an expression of lack of trust for Mary to seek such evidence than it is for us to study the evidence for our faith. It is always good to examine the evidences God offers to support our faith.

As Mary entered the house of Zacharias and Elizabeth she greeted Elizabeth, "And it happened, when Elizabeth heard the greeting of Mary, that the babe leaped in her womb." The term "babe," here used to designate John while he was still a fetus in Elizabeth's womb, is the same word employed to describe Jesus after He was born. (Luke 2:12,16) It means "*unborn child, embryo…. baby, infant.*" (Arndt & Gingrich. 146) The Holy Spirit used the same word to designate both a fetus and an infant. The unborn child, thus, is an infant, a baby, not just a growth. That babe inside Elizabeth experienced the human emotion of joy. (Luke 1:44) A fetus can also experience human pain. When a woman chooses to abort her unborn child, she has not simply chosen to remove an annoying growth, she has chosen to kill her baby.

Elizabeth's joyful greeting to Mary was faith building indeed!

> *Blessed are you among women, and blessed is the fruit of your womb!*
> *But why is this granted to me, that the mother of my Lord should come to me?*
> *For indeed, as soon as the voice of your greeting sounded in my ears, the babe leaped in my womb for joy.*
> *Blessed is she who believed, for there will be a fulfillment of those things which were told her from the Lord.* (Luke 1:42–45)

More than she could have imagined, Mary received the faith building encouragement she needed. Godly women should always be of such support to one another.

Mary's beautiful response is one of the great statements of faith of the New Testament, and is in reality an Old Testament psalm and one of the few examples of poetry in the New Testament.

> *And Mary said: "My soul magnifies the Lord,*
> *And my spirit has rejoiced in God my Savior.*
> *For He has regarded the lowly state of His maidservant;*
> *For behold, henceforth all generations will call me blessed.*
> *For He who is mighty has done great things for me,*
> *And holy is His name.*
> *And His mercy is on those who fear Him*
> *from generation to generation.*

*He has shown strength with His arm;
He has scattered the proud in the imagination of their hearts.
He has put down the mighty from their thrones,
And exalted the lowly.
He has filled the hungry with good things,
And the rich He has sent away empty.
He has helped His servant Israel,
In remembrance of His mercy,
As He spoke to our fathers,
To Abraham and to his seed forever."* (Luke 1:46–55)

As is a primary characteristic of great faith, Mary was thankful to God for His blessings, and she expressed her thankfulness through praise and thanksgiving. She glorified the Lord for His blessings to her personally in having regard for her in her humble condition (verses 46–48); for His great attributes of power, holiness and mercy demonstrated in what He had done for her (verses 49–50); for His awesome power manifested in overthrowing the wicked and proud (verses 51–53); and for His merciful remembrance of His people Israel and His promise to their fathers of the long awaited Messiah, the Seed of Abraham. (verses 54–55) When the Lord chose the human vessel to bring His Christ into the world, He passed over the blue blooded women of wealthy, proud families and chose a humble, poor, rustic maiden from the far away hills of Galilee. In the kingdom that the Christ would establish, the humble are exalted and the proud are abased. (Matthew 5:3; Luke 14:7–11) Earthly riches may be a hindrance in the Master's kingdom rather than the guarantee of honor and advancement that they are in the nations of men. (Mark 10:17–25; James 5:1–6)

Mary's song of praise is similar to the song Hannah, the mother of Samuel, sang when God granted her the son she prayed for. (1 Samuel 2:1–10) They both were sung by humble, thankful women in gratitude for a promised son. Each psalm is thoroughly feminine. They both praise the Lord for His special mercy to them, for His great power, and for the fact that He humbles the proud and exalts the lowly. Both hymns express complete trust in the Lord.

Mary was a humble woman with great faith. Her faith was expressed in thanksgiving and praise. Through her lips flowed, not ribald songs of the world, not gossip about her neighbors, but a song of thanksgiving and praise. The joy of faith finds expression in hymns of praise and thanksgiving. (James 5:13) Is it any wonder God highly favored her?

Matthew 1:18–25

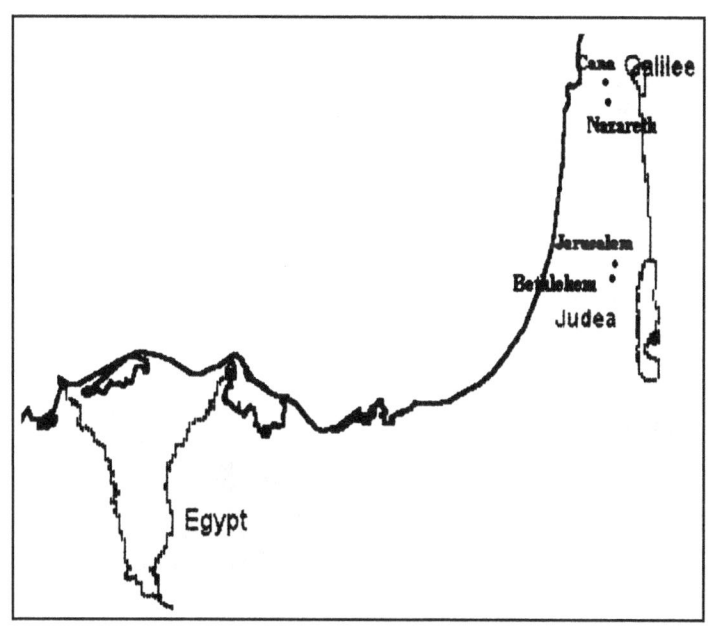

When Mary returned to Nazareth from visiting her cousin Elizabeth, she was three months pregnant. (Luke 1:56) Soon her pregnancy could not be hidden. When Joseph, her espoused husband learned she was with child, he decided to secretly divorce her. To his mind and to that of any not familiar with the miraculous facts, she was guilty of adultery. Joseph had the right to have her put to death, but he was merciful and did not desire to bring the full weight of the law against Mary. But at the same time he was righteous and needed to protect his good name. He could have publicly divorced her, thus exposing her to ridicule, clearing his own name, and exacting revenge for the wrong he had endured. (cf. Deuteronomy 24:1) Joseph expressed both his righteousness and mercy in his determination to obtain a secret divorce, thus protecting Mary from public ridicule while protecting his own good name. But an angel of God appeared to Joseph in a dream and revealed the true nature of the case. The Son Mary was to bear was conceived by the power of the Holy Spirit, His name would be called "Jesus," and His birth was in fulfillment of the prophecy of Isaiah 7:14 that a virgin would bear a Son and His name would be "Immanuel," i.e., "God with us." Joseph obeyed all that God commanded him, in that he took Mary to be his wife, did not have sexual relations with her until after Christ was born, and named the child "Jesus."

The man Mary agreed to marry was worthy to raise the Son of God. He was righteous, merciful, and obedient, even to accepting ridicule himself from unbelievers who would imagine he had fathered a child outside wedlock. When any young woman accepts the proposal to marriage of the man she hopes to wed, she has chosen the father of her children. Will he be the kind of father her children deserve? (Ephesians 6:4) A virtuous woman seeks to marry a virtuous man.

When Mary accepted the role of the mother of the Christ, she accepted the risk of being put to death for supposedly being an adulteress, losing her husband, and being ridiculed by unbelievers for the remainder of her life. Obedient faith courageously accepts the pain and ridicule that submission to God's will brings from an unbelieving world.

Think of all the trouble Mary's pregnancy caused her. She is pregnant out of wedlock. She is engaged to be married, but her fiancee is not the father of her baby. She was not at all at fault in the pregnancy; she was overpowered. Her fiancee is very morally strict and careful for his good name, and she can expect him to break off their engagement. She lives in a society where women who are pregnant out of wedlock can expect severe ridicule and maybe even be put to death. Her pregnancy could bring her sorrow and shame the rest of her life. If her fiancee does marry her, they are in poverty already and certainly don't need another mouth to feed. If Mary had selfishly thought only of her own temporal happiness, as many young men and women do today, the Christ, the Savior of the world, would have been aborted.

Luke 2:1–7

Bethlehem

Probably no story is more universally known (and virtually universally misused and covered with tradition) than that of the birth of Jesus Christ. While Quirinius was procurator of Syria, the Roman province that included Galilee and Judea, Caesar Augustus, ruler of the Roman Empire, decreed a taxation throughout the Empire. This demanded a census. The Romans allowed the Jews to return to their ancestral cities to be enrolled. Thus, Joseph, a descendant of David, returned to Bethlehem, the home village of his famous ancestor, taking with him Mary, his espoused wife, who was at full term of her pregnancy. Finding no room in the caravan shelter, they were forced to stay with the animals in the stable. While they stayed there Mary delivered her first born child, wrapped him tightly in cloths, as was the Jewish custom, and laid him in the only bed available, a feeding trough.

Luke 2:8–20

The first witnesses of Christ were shepherds watching their flocks in the Judean hills at night. In a dazzling appearance, accompanied with songs of praise by a heavenly host, an angel of the Lord announced to the shepherds, "...there is born to you this day in the city of David a Savior, who is Christ the Lord." (Luke 2:11) They went to see the child and found him even as the angel had said. When they told their story widely, people marveled. The shepherds glorified and praised God. But Mary, true to her thoughtful character, took note of all that was said and done, pondering their meaning in her heart.

Luke 2:21–40

Jesus was "born under the law." (Galatians 4:4) The Mosaic law demanded that a son be circumcised on the eighth day and be brought to the priest on the fortieth day with a yearling lamb as a burnt sacrifice and a young pigeon or turtledove as a sin offering. Those too impoverished to offer a lamb could bring two pigeons or two doves. (Leviticus chapter 12) Joseph and Mary obeyed all God commanded them. On the eighth day they had the Child circumcised and named Him Jesus, as the angel charged them. At the end of the days of purification they brought the sacrifice of those in poverty. As they brought Jesus into the temple to obey all the law demanded, an elderly, devoted saint named Simeon, to whom the Lord had promised he would see the Christ and who had been directed there by the Holy Spirit, met them. He took Jesus into His arms, thanked God for allowing him to see the Christ, and prophesied of the Child's future. Amidst all the glorious things said about Jesus, one prophecy spoken to Mary was ominous, "Yes, a sword will pierce through your own soul also." (Luke 2:35) When a mother properly raises her son to serve God, the persecutions that the ungodly heap on him bring her deep sorrow. Then an aged, widowed prophetess named Anna also praised God and spoke about Christ to those in the temple. Joseph and Mary did everything the law demanded concerning the birth of their son. Not only did Mary render the obedience of passive submission to God's will for her, she also gave the active obedience of compliance with every demand of the law.

Matthew chapter two

Within the second year of Jesus' life (Matthew 2:16), astrologers followed a star from the East to Judea to worship the Child who "was born King of the Jews." (Matthew 2:2) Herod, afraid his rule over Judea would be overthrown, deviously asked the wise men, when they located the child, to bring him word. He pretended to desire to worship the Christ, when in reality he desired to kill him. After they were directed to Bethlehem, found Christ, worshiped Him and presented Him royal presents, they were divinely instructed not to return to Herod. Joseph was warned in a dream to flee Herod for the Child's safety, and he obediently took Mary and Jesus to Egypt. Herod, enraged by the failure of his plot, had all the male children around Bethlehem under two years old murdered. What a horrible atrocity! What a beast Herod was! But was he any worse than America, where 1.5 million unborn babies are killed annually? When Joseph was directed to return from Egypt, hearing that Archelaus, the son of Herod reigned in Judea, he took Mary and Jesus to Nazareth, where Jesus grew up.

Luke 2:41–50

Nazareth

All Jewish men were required to appear before the altar of God during three great festivals of the law, one of which was Passover. (Deuteronomy 16:16) Jewish women were not under obligation to attend these festivals. Mary set a good example before her children of devotion to God beyond even the demand of the law by attending the Passover feast with her husband annually. Jewish custom considered a boy a "son of the law" and personally obligated to observe the law when He turned twelve. Thus, when Jesus was twelve, Joseph, Mary, and Jesus all attended the Passover in Jerusalem. Unknown to Mary and Joseph, Jesus remained behind in the temple while Mary and Joseph returned to Nazareth, thinking He was, as would be the custom of young people, visiting in another part of their traveling party. Only after they had been gone a full day did they realize He was missing, and they anxiously returned to Jerusalem and looked for Him for three days before finding Him in the most obvious place—the temple, where He amazed the renowned rabbis with His insight into the law. Mary, in obvious consternation, rebuked her Son, "Son, why have You done this to us? Look, Your father and I have sought You anxiously." (Luke 2:48) Jesus simply replied, "Why did you seek Me? Did you not know that I must be about My Father's business?" (Luke 2:49) Of all people, Mary should have understood that her Son, the Son of God, had divine business of His divine Father to attend to, but neither Mary nor Joseph understood His statement.

Luke 2:51

"Then He went down with them and came to Nazareth, and was subject to them, but His mother kept all these things in her heart."

Though Jesus was the divine Son of God, He was also the Son of man, and in His humanity, as a teenager, He was subject to His mother. Mary remained the same as always: a quiet, thoughtful, woman, pondering the meaning of all the wonderful sayings and events that were so much a part of her life.

No couple were ever entrusted with a weightier responsibility than were Mary and Joseph, when God chose them to raise His Son to maturity. The Lord gave Manoah and his wife a son to raise to be God's servant (Judges 13:1–14), but they were not as trustworthy as Joseph and Mary in their stewardship. Joseph and Mary not only cared for and protected Jesus from harm, they brought Him up to obey them and His Father. They were faithful stewards of the wonderful treasure God gave them. Every couple blessed with children are entrusted with treasures from God. Those children come to us free from the taint of sin. (Matthew 19:14) When they leave our homes, are they still free from sin? Are we faithful in our stewardship as parents?

John 2:1–12

The next recorded incident in the lives of Mary and Her divine Son occurred eighteen years later, as they, along with the Lord's twelve disciples, attended a wedding feast in Cana of Galilee. When the wedding party ran out of wine, a social catastrophe that brought deep concern to Mary's feminine heart, Mary tried to get Christ to remedy the situation by simply informing him, "They have no wine." (John 2:3) Apparently she wanted Him to both supply the needed wine and, in the process, reveal His divinity. The Lord replied, "Woman, what does your concern have to do with Me? My hour has not yet come" (John 2:4) Jesus was now an adult and had entered His ministry. He respected His mother, as the law demanded and as He Himself demands of us (Exodus 20:12; Ephesians 6:2–3), but it was not time for Him to reveal He was the Son of God, a fact He fully confirmed by His resurrection. (Romans 1:4) Mary demonstrated her faith in her Son by telling the attendants to do whatever He said. He did perform the miracle of turning water to wine, His first miracle, but He rebuked His mother for interfering with His public ministry. Mothers of preachers should resist the temptation to meddle in theirs sons' public work.

Matthew 12:46–50; Mark 3:31–35; Luke 8:19–21

We next encounter Mary during the Lord's Galilean ministry. She came, along with His brothers, to attempt to see Him while he was preaching to a multitude. They thought their business with him was so urgent that they had the gall to interrupt His sermon. His brothers did not believe in Him at this time. (John 7:5) They were seeking to seize Him and take Him home, thinking He was insane and would bring harm to Himself by incurring the wrath of the Jewish rulers. (Mark 3:21) Although Mary knew who Jesus was, apparently her concern for her Son's safety caused her to join their ill advised attempt. Mary and Jesus' brothers earned His rebuke, as He asserted that His real kinsmen were His disciples. The loving concern of a mother should not cause her to interfere with the work of a devoted man of God, though he may be her son, and she may have real reason to fear for his carnal welfare.

John 19:25–27

But Mary's devotion to her Son never wavered. As He hung dying on the cross, she stood, heartbroken and undoubtedly greatly confused, with the other women who remained after the men had fled. Indeed, how a sword must have pierced her gentle soul when the rough spear pierced His side.

In loving devotion to His mother, the Lord showed the honor a son should have for his mother. Apparently she was now a widow. As he experienced the agony of the death of the cross, He solemnly made arrangement for the care of His mother after He was gone. One of the men, His beloved disciple John, yet remained at the foot of the cross. Seeing John, Jesus said to Mary, "Woman, behold your son!" Then to John He said, "Behold your mother!" "And from that hour that disciple took her to his own home." No son ever showed greater love, devotion, and honor to his mother.

Calvary

No greater example has ever been recorded of the honor a son should bestow upon his mother than this touching scene. One cannot allow religious contributions to replace honor to parents. (Mark 7:6–13) If the most important ministry the earth has ever known and the death on the cross did not deter Jesus from honoring His mother by seeing that she was provided for, surely no preacher should think his work for God will excuse him from fulfilling this fundamental obligation. A man of God may travel ten thousand miles from home and be involved in fruitful work leading the lost to Christ, edifying God's people, and defending the faith, but it is still his responsibility to honor his mother.

Acts 1:14

But how happy the last, brief inspired reference to Mary, the mother of Jesus. There in the company of 120 disciples who waited in faith for the Lord Jesus Christ to send the Holy Spirit was Mary and the brothers of Jesus, her formerly disbelieving sons (and what hope this offers to mothers with unbelieving children). She had made mistakes, she often failed to comprehend the profound words and events that swirled around her, but her faith was true. Her years of quiet, thoughtful pondering at last had come to fruition. Now she was kin to Jesus in a higher, far more important way. Now she understood. Now she was His disciple.

Conclusion

Indeed Mary was highly favored of God. She was chosen to be the earthen vessel through whom the Son of God would come into the world, and who would raise Him as her own Son. What a trust was committed to her. And she was faithful to that trust.

Her recorded life reveals qualities of character that demonstrate why God chose her for such a signal honor. This peasant girl from Galilee exemplifies moral purity; ready faith; humble submission to God's will; a quiet, thoughtful nature; thanksgiving to and praise of God; moral courage; and active obedience to all God's law. Though her motherly instinct and lack of understanding caused her to draw rebukes from her divine Son, her faith remained true. She, along with her formerly disbelieving sons, was a part of that company of the original disciples of the risen Lord. She was even more highly favored by receiving the spiritual kinship to the Lord that transcends all earthly ties.

Questions

I. List of Passages Used in This Lesson (Read each passage and be able to discuss its meaning and its application to the lesson.)

Luke 1:26–38
Deuteronomy 22:23-24
Isaiah 9:6-7
Genesis 17:15-19
Genesis 18:9-12,14
Genesis 21:1-7
Hebrews 11:11
Luke 2:8–20
Luke 2:21-40
Galatians 4:4
Leviticus chapter 12
Matthew chapter 2
Luke 2:41-51
John 2:1-12

Luke 1:39-56
Matthew 5:3
Luke 14:7-11
Mark 10:17-25
James 5:1-6
1 Samuel 2:1-10
James 5:13
Matthew 1:18-25
Deuteronomy 24:1
Ephesians 6:4
Isaiah 7:14
Luke 2:1–7

Exodus 20:12
Ephesians 6:2-3
Romans 1:4
Matthew 12:46-50
Mark 3:31-35
Luke 8:19-21
John 7:5
Mark 3:21
John 19:25-27
Acts 1:14
Mark 7:6-13

II. Terms to Define

1. Isaac

2. babe

3. Immanuel

III. Fact Questions

Tell the story of:

1. Gabriel appearing to Mary.

2. Mary's visit to Elizabeth.

3. the announcement of Jesus' birth to Joseph.

4. the birth of Christ.

5. the shepherds.

6. Jesus' circumcision and presentation in the temple.

7. the childhood of Jesus before He was twelve.

8. the trip to Jerusalem when Jesus was twelve.

9. the youth of Jesus after He was twelve.

10. the wedding feast in Cana of Galilee.

11. the visit of Mary and her sons to Jesus.

12. Mary at the foot of the cross.

13. the last biblical reference to Mary.

IV. Thought Questions

1. How serious was espousal in Jewish society?

2. How highly was Mary favored by God?

3. How great would her Child be?

4. How great was Mary's faith?

5. Did she evidence any doubt?

6. Is a fetus a person or a growth?

7. Is abortion the removal of a growth or the killing of a child?

8. How did Elizabeth strengthen Mary's faith?

9. Analyze Mary's poetic response to Elizabeth's greeting.

10. What characteristic of the kingdom of heaven did her song exhibit?

11. What did this psalm show about Mary's faith?

12. How does it resemble the song of Hannah?

13. What kind of man was Joseph?

14. What lesson should this teach young women?

15. How did Mary's role demand courage?

16. Do godly women show courage when they submit to God's will in difficult situations? Explain your answer.

17. Does the birth of Jesus teach us any lessons about abortion?

18. How did Mary and Joseph demonstrate obedience to the law of God?

19. How did Mary and Joseph set a good example for us as parents?

20. Did Mary improperly interfere in the ministry of Jesus?

21. How does the relationship between Mary and Her divine Son illustrate the relationship between a mother and her grown son who preaches the gospel?

22. Does the story of Mary end happily? How so?

V. Discussion

The class should compile a list of the character traits Mary exhibited and discuss how they can incorporate these into their own lives or, in case of bad qualities, avoid them.

Work Cited

Arndt, W.F. and F.W. Gingrich. **A Greek-English Lexicon of the New Testament.**

TEACH Services, Inc.
P U B L I S H I N G

We invite you to view the complete
selection of titles we publish at:
www.TEACHServices.com

We encourage you to write us
with your thoughts about this,
or any other book we publish at:
info@TEACHServices.com

TEACH Services' titles may be purchased in
bulk quantities for educational, fund-raising,
business, or promotional use.
bulksales@TEACHServices.com

Finally, if you are interested in seeing
your own book in print, please contact us at:
publishing@TEACHServices.com

We are happy to review your manuscript at no charge.